MICROBREWS

MICROBREWS

A Guide to America's Best New Beers and Breweries

Matthew Zimmermann
&
Chad B. Stice

Andrews and McMeel

A Universal Press Syndicate Company
Kansas City

Zimmerman, Matthew.
  Microbrews: a guide to America's best new beers and breweries /
  Matthew Zimmerman & Chad B. Stice. p. cm.   ISBN 0-8362-2171-0 (pb)
    1. Brewing industry–United States–Directories. 2. Beer industry–United
    States–Directories. 3. Microbreweries–United States–Directories.
    I. Stice, Chad B. II. Title.
      HD9397.U52Z56 1996   96-18812
      338.7'66342'02573–dc20   CIP

Layout and Graphic Design

      Third Degree Graphic Design — Kevin J. Capizzi & Daniel J. Stahl

Digital Prepress

      Alpha 21 – Creative Electronic Color Prepress

Attention: Schools and Businesses
Andrews and McMeel books are available at quantity discounts with bulk purchase for educational, business, or sales promotional use. For information, please write to Special Sales Department, Andrews and McMeel, 4520 Main Street, Kansas City, Missouri 64111.

The authors wish to acknowledge the Zimmermann family, the Stice family, Sarah Zimmermann, J.P. Frisone, Joe Rogowski, and Dung Cao, whose patience and support made this book possible.

INTRODUCTION

As you walk back into the house, your shirt sticks to your back, your hair is dripping wet, and fresh-cut grass clings to your shoes. Why is it that the first thing you go for is a cold beer, not a shower? This, and a thousand other examples, tell us that Americans don't just like their beer—they love it. And because of this passion, the American beer revolution is in full swing.

Our infatuation with imported beers has been replaced by a new passion—domestically produced microbrewed beers. Micro-mania is sweeping the states like wildfire, and beer drinkers are now blessed with a wide variety of new tastes gracing their local beer shelves or favorite tap handles. In *Microbrews*, we hope to expose beer drinkers all over America to some of the new options available and provide an entertaining guide for your quest for new tastes.

We are not professional beer tasters or brewers. There are many organizations that annually pin their coveted awards on beers and breweries, and supply expert judgment on the best of the new brews. We are simply consumers who like drinking beer and judging for ourselves which brews we like best. Let's just say that beer is our hobby, and in *Microbrews*, we decided to share our collection with you!

We also believe in the old adage that a picture is worth a thousand words, so we combined the slick collectible labels and catchy names of the new microbrewed beers with descriptions provided by the brewers themselves. Beer is enjoyed by people of all social groups, and the featured labels provide a lavish visual guide to help anyone on a journey through the ever-evolving world of microbrews. The beers are listed alphabetically by label name, and there is an index of breweries at the back of the book.

Throughout the compilation of this book, we were amazed and delighted by the brewers' pride in their products. The definition of "microbrewed" beers is the subject of a hot debate that we chose not to enter in this book. We prefer to simply acknowledge the proud American breweries that are endlessly stretching the boundaries of beer color, aroma, and taste far beyond those set by the giant-volume producers, who shall remain nameless.

We hope this book is both entertaining and informative. If you haven't tried many micro-brewed beers, look for them in your area and sample a few—you won't regret it. If you are an experienced "micromaniac," you can use this book as a reference to the gems you've missed, while guiding friends to new beers that delight the palate.

Sit back, sip a cold one, and enjoy!

Beer is living proof
that God loves us.
Ben Franklin

Abita Bock

The Abita Brewing Company
P.O. Box 762
Abita Springs, LA
   70420
(800) 737-2311

Other Beers:
Abita Amber
Abita Golden
Abita Red Ale
Abita Wheat
Turbodog
Fall Fest
Purple Haze
XXX-Mas Ale

Abita Bock is the first of The Abita Brewing Company's seasonal beers, and is available from January 1 to March 15. Brewed with Yakima Perle hops and British two-row and caramel malts, Abita Bock is similar to German Maibock in its high malt content, full body, and high alcohol content. It is very popular for Twelfth Night celebrations and subsequent Carnival and Jazzfest parties.

Adler Brau Extra Special Bitter

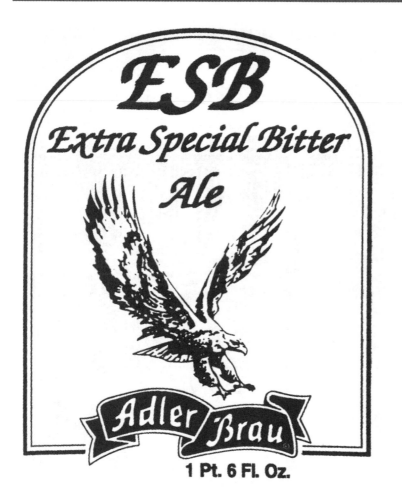

Appleton Brewing Company
1004 S. Olde Oneida St.
Appleton, WI 54915
(414) 735-0507

Other Beers:
Eagle Lager
Cherry Creek
Mosquito Pilsner
Marquette Export
  Lager
Tailgate Amber
E.S.B.
Classic Porter
Oatmeal Stout

Appleton Brewing Company began brewing in July 1989, and soon revived the Adler Brau name from the previously closed George Walter Brewery. The brewery is in the historic "Between the Locks" building, the original home of the Muench Brewery, and prides itself on producing beers with a bold, hearty body and clean, crisp finish. The Adler Brau line of handcrafted beers has won numerous medals at many of the premier beer judgings in America. It is brewed using only barley malt, hops, yeast, water, and a dedication to brew the finest beer available.

Alaskan Brewing & Bottling Company
5429 Shaune Dr.
Juneau, AK 99801
(907) 780-5866

Other Beers:
Alaskan Pale
Alaskan Frontier

Voted best beer in the nation at the 1988 Great American Beer Festival® by the Consumer Preference Poll, Alaskan Amber is based on a Gold Rush era recipe. This richly malty, copper-colored *Altbier* is skillfully hopped for a well-balanced, lingering finish. Alaskan Amber was honored with gold medals in the alt category at the 1987, 1988, and 1990 Great American Beer Festivals®. Celebrating ten years of producing award-winning beers for Alaska, the Alaskan Brewing & Bottling Company remains committed to a future of producing the finest specialty beers from only the highest-quality ingredients. The Juneau microbrewery, founded in 1986, is Alaska's oldest operating brewery and produces beers for the adventurer in all of us.

Alaskan Frontier

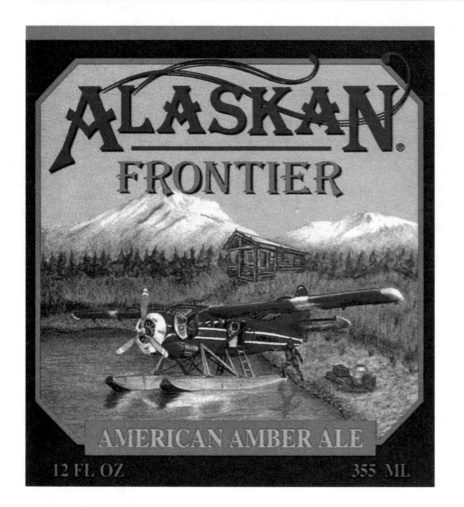

**Alaskan Brewing &
Bottling Company**
5429 Shaune Dr.
Juneau, AK 99801
(907) 780-5866

Other Beers:
Alaskan Pale
Alaskan Amber

This popular Alaskan Seasonal joined Amber and Pale as a year-'round product in 1996. Brewed in the robust style of a German *Festbier*, Alaskan Frontier is richly malted with a crisp, hoppy finish. Originally called Alaskan Autumn Ale, this beer has won five medals in the American Amber Ale category at the Great American Beer Festival®—gold medals in 1991, 1994, and 1995 and silver medals in 1989 and 1990. Celebrating ten years of producing award-winning beers for Alaska, the Alaskan Brewing & Bottling Company remains committed to a future of producing the finest specialty beers from only the highest-quality ingredients. The Juneau microbrewery, founded in 1986, is Alaska's oldest operating brewery and produces beers for the adventurer in all of us.

Alcatraz Stout Ale

**San Francisco
Brewing Company**
155 Columbus Ave.
San Francisco, CA
  94133
(415) 434-3344

Other Beers:
Emperor Norton
  Lager

San Francisco Brewing Company uses lots of roasted black and amber barley malt in Alcatraz Stout Ale. The roasted malts create a complex flavor dominated by the character of black barley malt. Imported and domestic whole-leaf hops heighten the rich taste. Brewed about a mile from Alcatraz in the North Beach section of San Francisco. The perfect beer for those foggy nights when Alcatraz's searchlight lights up the darkness.

Alimony Ale

Buffalo Bill's Brewery
Box 510
Hayward, CA
94543-0510
(510) 538-9500

Other Beers:
Diaper Pale Ale
Pumpkin Ale
Tasmanian Devil
Hearty Ale
Billy Bock
Krambic

The CPA for Bill Owens, the brewmaster of Buffalo Bills Brewery, was going through a bitter divorce when the idea of Alimony Ale was born. It was to be the bitterest beer in America. To accomplish this, the hopping rate on an Amber beer was tripled from four pounds to twelve. The Ale at this level became floral. Its BU (bitterness units) reached 72. Most American beers are only 16 BUs. This beer captures the essence of its namesake.

Alleycat Amber Ale

Lost Coast Brewery
123 W. Third Street
Eureka, CA 95501
(707) 445-4485

Other Beers:
Downtown Brown

Alleycat Amber Ale is a full-flavored amber ale made with roasted caramel malt. Richly colored and medium-bodied, amber ale is an assertive blend of malts with a sprightly cascade of hops. This high-quality, handcrafted beer is brewed fresh in the Humboldt Nation and may be enjoyed at the Lost Coast Brewery and Café in downtown Eureka, California, or in the comfort of your own home.

American Amber Ale

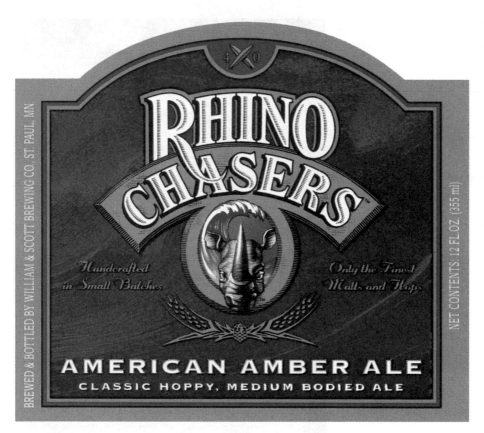

William & Scott Brewing Company
2130 Main St.
Suite 250
Huntington Beach, CA
  92648
(800) 788-HORN

Other Beers:
Dark Roasted Läger
Peach Honey Wheat
Winterful

American Amber Ale is the flagship brand of Rhino Chasers. This award-winning American ale combines the crisp, refreshing characteristics of a world-class lager beer with the rich, full-bodied flavor of a traditional American-style amber ale. This is a great brew to enjoy anytime. This beer won a silver medal in the Düsseldorf-style category at the 1993 Great American Beer Festival®. If you'd like to try an award-winning Rhino Chasers ale, it's best to have it on draft. It's easy to tell which establishments carry Rhino Chasers on draft—just look for the rhino horn tap handle at a tavern near you.

Cherryland Brewery Ltd.
341 N. 3rd Ave.
Sturgeon Bay, WI 54235
(414) 743-1945

Other Beers:
Silver Rail
Golden Rail
Cherry Rail
Door County Raspberry
   Bier

Apple Bach beer is a Maibock brewed with apple juice. This tasty brew is golden in appearance with a distinct apple cider finish. Cherryland Brewery was founded in 1987 and is on northeastern Wisconsin's Door County Peninsula. The brewery is open year-'round for daily tours, 9:00 A.M. to 5:00 P.M.

9

Arches Amber Ale

EDDIE McSTIFFS

Amber Ale

No Preservatives, No Additives

KEEP REFRIGERATED
Drink Within 30 Days
Contents: 1Pint, 6 Fluid Ounces
Made from: Malted Barley, Hops, Yeast, Pure Desert Water

Brewed and Bottled by Eddie McStiff's Inc.
Moab, Utah 84532

COPYRIGHT 1991

Eddie McStiff's
57 S. Main
Moab, UT 84532
(801) 259-2337

Other Beers:
Lime Ale
Jalapeno Beer
Blueberry Stout
Canyon Cream Ale
McStiff's Wheat
  Beer
McStiff's Stout
Raspberry Wheat
Blueberry Wheat
Arches Amber Ale
Chestnut Brown
Cherry Wheat
Spruce Beer
Orange Blossom

Eddie McStiff's Arches Amber Ale is your neighborhood English bitter. Copper-colored with the unmistakable flavor of imported British Carastan malt and a finish of Perle hops, Arches Amber Ale is lightly carbonated and ready to go a session in the pub. Eddie McStiff's was founded in March 1991, in Moab, Utah, the heart of Utah's canyonland.

Crown City Brewery

300 S. Raymond Ave.
Pasadena, CA 91105
(818) 577-5548

Other Beers:

Mt. Wilson Wheat

Black Cloud Oatmeal
Stout

Yorkshire Porter

Dragon Anniversary
Ale

Oom Pah Pah
Oktoberfest

Black Forest
Dunkelweizen

Doo Dah Apan-Ale

Father Christmas
Wassail Ale

Irish Ale

Black Rose Irish Stout

Black Bear Stout

Midsummer's Night
Stout

Spring Is Here Bock

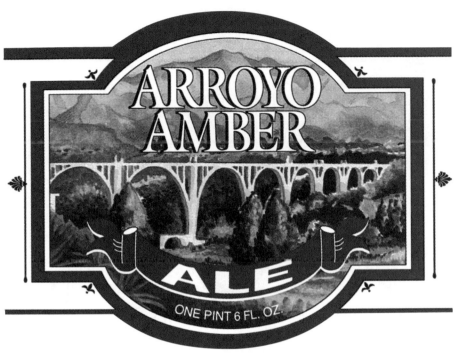

Arroyo Amber Ale is an American amber-style ale inspired by the English pale ales. Arroyo Amber Ale contains carapils, caramel malt, and a pinch of chocolate malt to produce its nutty flavor. The fruity finish and pleasing aroma from Cascade, Nugget, and Mt. Hood hops round out the flavor profile of this medium-brown-colored ale. Arroyo Amber Ale goes well with hearty foods, meats, and ethnic dishes as well.

Atlas Amber Ale

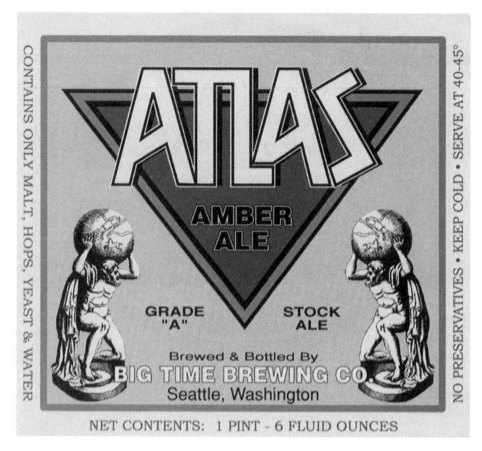

Big Time Brewing Company
4133 University
    Way, N.E.
Seattle, WA 98105
(206) 545-4509

Other Beers:
Coal Creek Porter
Bhagwan's Best
    India Pale Ale
Old Wooly
    Barleywine Ale
Prime Time Pale Ale

Atlas Amber Ale is Big Time's most popular beer. Its mixture of pale, crystal, Munich, and light dextrin malts, with just a few pounds of roasted barley, give it a robust malt flavor and a rich, bronze color. Three distinctive northwestern hops (Chinook, Cascade, and Centennial) also give Atlas Amber Ale an aggressive hoppy character.

**Breckenridge
Brewery**
2220 Blake St.
Denver, CO 80205
(303) 297-3644

**Other Breckenridge
Beers:**
Mountain Wheat
India Pale Ale
Oatmeal Stout
Ballpark Brown Ale

Breckenridge Brewery's Avalanche is a medium-bodied amber ale that is malty rich and lightly sweet. It's brewed with caramel malts and a perfect balance of Chinook, Willamette, Tettnang, and Hallertau hops. The brewery is across from Coors Field and was the first brewer in Colorado to bottle and sell their brews in the now famous 22-ounce "Bomber" bottles.

Bachelor Bitter

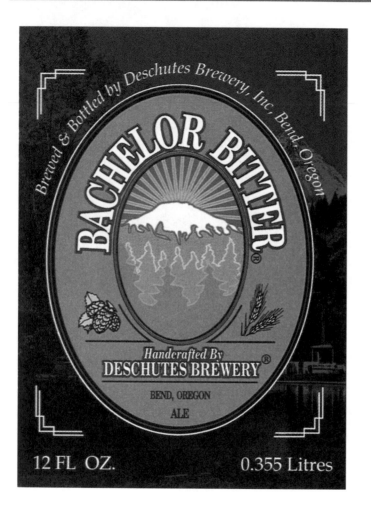

Deschutes Brewery
901 S.W. Simpson Ave.
Bend, OR 97702
(541) 385-8606

Other Beers:
Deschutes Brewery
  Jubelale
Black Butte Porter
Cascade Golden Ale
Obsidian Stout

Deschutes Brewery's Bachelor Bitter is a British-style "best bitter," coppery in color and robust in flavor. This is the perfect ale for the British ale enthusiast or for the person looking for more body and complexity in his or her favorite ale.

Bad Frog Beer

Bad Frog Brewery Company
2644 M-33 N.
P.O. Box 310
Rose City, MI 48654
(517) 685-2990

Bad Frog Beer is a rich, golden-amber lager carefully made according to the German Purity Law of 1516. Bad Frog uses specially selected two-row barley malt, Munich malt, caramel 60 malt, and dextrin malt along with a careful blend of Cluster and Perle hops in an infusion-mashing system. The brew is then fermented with a unique yeast strain from the brewing academy Doemens in Munich, Germany. Fermentation takes approximately seven days, after which the beer is cooled and stored at 32°F for a minimum of twenty-one days. This long, cold maturation time is what gives Bad Frog Beer its smooth but distinct, rich character. See why Bad Frog is one of the fastest growing micro-beers in the country. Bad Frog Beer, the beer's so good . . . it's bad!

Baderbräu Bock Beer

Pavichevich Brewing Company
383 Romans Rd.
Elmhurst, IL 60126
(708) 617-5252

Other Beers:
Baderbräu Pilsener
Baderbräu Winterfest
Baderbräu Amber
  Ale

Baderbräu Bock Beer has been a gold medal winner in beer events around the country. It is a European-style bock beer that is fire-brewed in a copper brewkettle to "carmelize" the beer for further flavor enhancement. This beer also conforms to the German Purity Law of 1516, which allows only malted barley, hops, yeast, and water as ingredients. Brewery tours are available to the public on weekends.

Balcones Fault Pale Malt

Hill Country Brewing & Bottling Company
730 Shady Ln.
Austin, TX 78702
(512) 385-9111

Other Beers:
Balcones Fault Red
  Granite

Balcones Fault Pale Malt is a traditional English pale ale with distinct hop flavor and aroma. Hill Country Brewing & Bottling Company, the only microbrewery in Austin, Texas, has brewed this handcrafted bitter since March 1995. You have to come to Texas to sample this beer, which is as refreshing as Hamilton's Pool on the label. It's our fault!

Balcones Fault Red Granite

Hill Country Brewing & Bottling Company
730 Shady Ln.
Austin, TX 78702
(512) 385-9111

Other Beers:
Balcones Fault Pale Malt

Balcones Fault Red Granite is an English-style brown ale brewed by Hill Country Brewing & Bottling Company, the only microbrewery in Austin, Texas. The label pictures a red granite mountain in the scenic hill country west of Austin. If you can't find Red Granite in your hometown, check out the Texas Spirits Saloon in Rio Medina, Texas.

**Breckenridge
Brewery**
2220 Blake St.
Denver, CO 80205
(303) 297-3644

**Other Breckenridge
Beers:**
Mountain Wheat
India Pale Ale
Oatmeal Stout
Avalanche

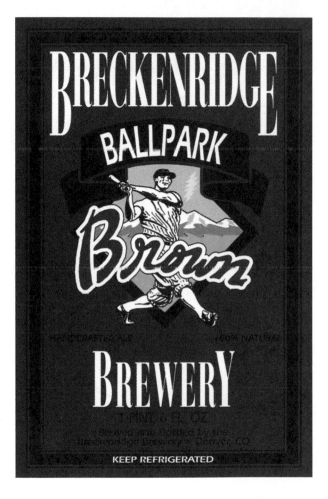

Breckenridge Brewery's Ballpark Brown Ale is a complex, balanced brown ale that is copper in color with a nutty-sweet malt character. It is brewed with two-row pale, Munich, roasted barley and chocolate malts complemented by Washington State Perle and Hallertau hops. The brewery is across from Coors Field and was the first brewer in Colorado to bottle and sell its brews in the now famous 22-ounce "Bomber" bottles.

Bambino Ale

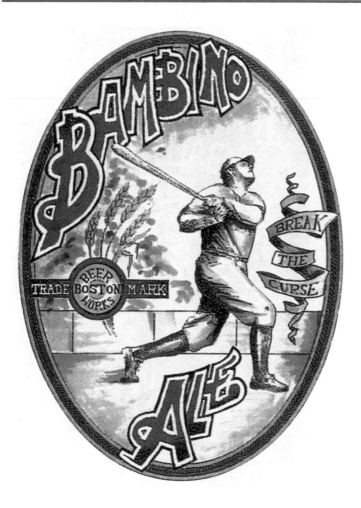

Boston Beer Works®
61 Brookline Ave.
Boston, MA 02215
(617) 536-BEER

Other Beers:
Fenway Pale Ale
Hercules Strong Ale
Victory Bock
Boston Red
Centennial Alt
Kenmore Kölsch
Beantown Nut
  Brown Ale
Buckeye Oatmeal
  Stout
Curley's Irish Stout
B.B.W. Eisbock Lager

The ill-fated sale of Babe Ruth to the Yankees after the 1919 season commenced the Boston Red Sox' infamous string of postseason bad luck. Every Red Sox fan understands the enormity of the "Curse of the Bambino," and Bambino Ale is Boston Beer Works' response. A clean, refreshing, golden light ale, it's perfect for a day at the park. Enjoy a Bambino Ale and help break the "curse"! Boston Beer Works is at 61 Brookline Avenue, directly across the street from historic Fenway Park, in the heart of Kenmore Square.

Bar Room Honey Red Ale

Brewski's Brewing Company
142 Arena St.
El Segundo, CA
  90245
(800) 901-2500

Other Beers:
Bar Room Ale
Bar Room Blonde
  Lager

Brewski's Bar Room Red Ale is a top-fermented red amber ale blessed with a variety of natural sweet honeys and balanced with American varieties of hops, producing a very complex balance of bitterness, flavor, and aroma. The malt varieties combined with natural honeys give this red amber ale a balanced, fruity, esoteric flavor.

Beehive Lager

Squatters Brewery
375 W. 200 S.
Salt Lake City, UT
 84101
(801) 328-2329

Other Beers:
Squatters Hefeweizen
Captain Bastard's
 Oatmeal Stout
Hop Head Red

Beehive Lager is a light, crisp Bohemian-style lager finished with Czech Saaz hops. Squatters Brewery found the demand for their fine ales and lagers growing faster than their brewing capacity. So in January 1994 they purchased the historic Henderson Building to expand their production. The brewery addition, Fuggles, has the ultimate capacity to produce 30,000 barrels a year and has begun supplying its brews to clubs, restaurants, ski resorts, and hotels along the Wasatch front.

Coophouse Brewery
2400 Industrial Ln.
 #350
Broomfield, CO 80020
(303) 466-3777

Other Beers:
Blue Suede Ale
Liver Lager

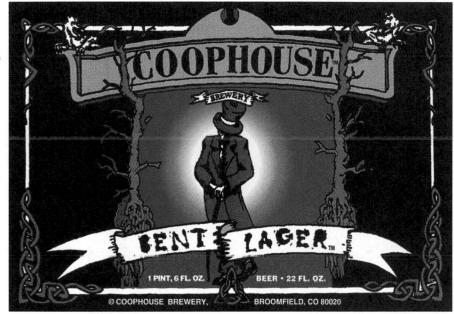

Bent Lager is Coophouse Brewery's version of an Oktoberfest-style brew, lightly hopped and complete with an exquisite malt finish. You're likely to Get Bent drinking this ghostly lager. Coophouse Brewery, in Broomfield, Colorado, has been brewing lagers and ales since March 1995. Coophouse Brewery brews in a tiny seven-barrel brewkettle, producing their righteous beer in extremely limited quantities.

Berkshire Ale

Berkshire Brewing Company
12 Railroad St.
South Deerfield, MA
  01373-0096
(413) 665-6600

Other Beers:
Steel Rail Extra Pale
  Ale
Drayman's Porter

Berkshire Ale is a traditional pale ale with a deep copper color, a caramel/malt flavor, and a very rich hop aroma and flavor. The brewery's goal is to produce clean, fresh, well-balanced ales in small batches. Berkshire is particularly proud of its flagship product, the Steel Rail Extra Pale Ale.

Yegua Creek Brewing Company
2920 N. Henderson Ave.
Dallas, TX 75206
(214) 824-BREW

Other Beers:
Tucker's Golden Wheat
Lucky Lady Lager
Xit Pilsner
Ice Haus Pale Ale
White Rock Red
O'Brien's Texas Stout
Sara's Brown Ale

Big D ESB (Extra Special Bitter) is darker than the brewery's pale ale but more forgiving in the hop category. Nice and easy going down makes it a real crowd-pleaser. Yegua Creek Brewing Company is housed in a seventy-year-old icehouse near downtown Dallas.

Big Shoulders Porter

Chicago Brewing Company
1830 N. Besly Ct.
Chicago, IL
  60622-1210
(312) 252-2739

Other Beers:
Legacy Lager
Heartland Weiss
  Beer
Legacy Red Ale

Chicago's Big Shoulders Porter, crafted as an authentic English-style porter, has received numerous awards, including a silver medal from the Beverage Testing Institute® in 1994. This award-winning beer is brewed and bottled by Chicago Brewing Company and has a smooth body with a creamy malt taste accented by chocolate and caramel malts.

Bigfoot Ale

Sierra Nevada Brewing Company
1075 E. 20th St.
Chico, CA 95928
(916) 893-3520

Other Sierra Nevada Beers:
Pale Bock
Summerfest
Celebration Ale
Porter
Pale Ale
Stout

BREWED & BOTTLED BY SIERRA NEVADA BREWING CO., CHICO, CA

Bigfoot Ale is an award-winning example of the English barleywine ale style. It boasts a dense, fruity bouquet; an extremely rich, intense, bittersweet palate; and a deep, reddish-brown color. This ale is superbly balanced between an almost overpowering maltiness and a wonderfully bittersweet hoppiness.

Black Butte Porter

Alc. 4.5% By Wt.

Brewed & Bottled by Deschutes Brewery, Inc, Bend, Oregon

BLACK BUTTE PORTER

Handcrafted By
DESCHUTES BREWERY
BEND, OREGON

12 FL OZ.   0.355 Litres

Deschutes Brewery
901 S.W. Simpson Ave.
Bend, OR 97702
(541) 385-8606

Other Beers:
Bachelor Bitter
Deschutes Brewery
    Jubelale
Cascade Golden Ale
Obsidian Stout

A century ago, a beer similar to Black Butte Porter was a staple of the deliverymen after whom it was named: If you didn't tip the guy, a "porter," you might find some of your luggage damaged on arrival at the local hostelry.

Brooklyn Brewery
118 N. 11th St.
Brooklyn, NY 11211
(718) 486-7422

Other Brooklyn Beers:
Brown Ale
East India Pale Ale
Brooklyn Lager

LIMITED BOTTLING—WINTER '94-'95

Black Chocolate Stout

12 FLUID OUNCES
BREWED AND BOTTLED BY THE BROOKLYN BREWERY, UTICA, N.Y.

At 500 barrels, the first run of this beer was the largest batch of imperial stout ever brewed in North America, brewed at the century-old F. X. Matt Brewing Company in Utica, New York. A ten-day primary fermentation is followed by at least two months of conditioning. Brooklyn Black Chocolate Stout is not filtered. Bottles are pasteurized to protect the freshness and extend the shelf life.

Black Jack Black & Tan

Wainwright Brewing Company
3410 Sassafras St.
Pittsburgh, PA
  15201-1321
(412) 682-7400

Other J. J. Wainwright's Beers:
Evil Eye Oktoberfest
Evil Eye Honey Brown
Evil Eye Ale

Black Jack Black & Tan is a handcrafted blend of dark, rich porter with a light pilsner to create a distinctively rich taste. Wainwright Brewing Company, founded in 1821, merged with twenty other breweries in 1899 as part of Pittsburgh Brewing Company. The recipes used today to brew Wainwright's beers are the original recipes that have been retrieved from the archives.

Left Hand Brewing Company

1265 Boston Ave.
Longmont, CO
   80501
(303) 772-0258

Other Beers:

Sawtooth Ale

Motherlode Golden
   Ale

Juju Ginger Ale

Jackman's American
   Pale Ale

Maid Marion
   Berry Ale

XXXmas Ale

Imperial Stout

A traditional London-style beer, Black Jack Porter highlights chocolate malt and Kent Goldings hops. Its slight initial sweetness quickly yields to the distinctive roastiness of the chocolate malt. Left Hand Brewing Company opened in January 1994. Their capacity is 8,000 barrels per year. Left Hand Brewing Company brews only the finest beer possible (it's their life). The brewery is on the banks of the mighty St. Vrain River.

Blackhook Porter

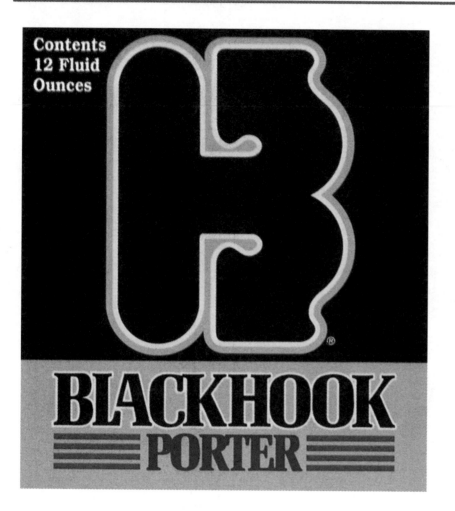

The Redhook Ale Brewery, Inc.
3400 Phinney Ave. N.
Seattle, WA 98103
(206) 548-8000

Other Beers:
Wheathook Ale
Redhook ESB
Ballard Bitter IPA
Redhook Rye
Extra Special Bitter
  Ale
Winterhook
  Christmas Ale
Redhook Double
  Black Stout

The addition of unmalted, roasted black barley gives this traditional London-style, top-fermenting black porter its distinctive flavor and dark ebony color. Its rich flavors, reminiscent of chocolate and coffee, are perfectly complemented by the bitterness of the hops. Naturally carbonated, Blackhook is a perfect match for eggplant parmesan, and goes well with red sauces, pasta, and oysters.

**Blue Hen Beer
Company, Ltd.**
P.O. Box 7077
Newark, DE
  19714-7077
(302) 737-8375

Other Beers:
Blue Hen Black
  & Tan

Blue Hen Beer is craft-brewed from the finest ingredients, including roasted barley malts and domestic and European hop varieties. The style of Blue Hen fits into the Continental Lager classification (i.e., Munich Helles Lager). Blue Hen Beer was judged in the 1994 World Beer Championships® as the world champion in the Munich Lager Class (number 1 in class) and awarded 87 points (of 100 possible) for a silver medal overall. Blue Hen Beer was again awarded a silver medal in the Munich Helles Class at the 1995 World Beer Championships®.

Blue Hen Black & Tan

Blue Hen Beer Company, Ltd.
P.O. Box 7077
Newark, DE
  19714-7077
(302) 737-8375

Other Beers:
Blue Hen Beer

Bravery in battle and the colorful gamecocks they carried with them earned Delaware's revolutionary militia the name "Fighting Blue Hens." A proprietary blend of the brewery's Blue Hen Lager and Porter, Blue Hen Black & Tan offers a mixture of two great products in one. This dark brew is not as heavy and intense as their porter, but remains full of flavor and character. Blue Hen Black & Tan is a nice, flavorful, malty-dark beer that was awarded a silver medal in the 1996 World Beer Championships®. Share in the history of America's first state and enjoy this fine brew offered to you in the memory and spirit of Delaware's "Fighting Blue Hens."

Blue Ridge Porter

Frederick Brewing Company
103 S. Carroll St.
Frederick, MD
  21701
(301) 694-7899

Other Blue Ridge Beers:
Golden Ale
Amber Lager
Wheat Beer
Subliminator
  Dopplebock
Hopfest
Cranberry Noel
Steeple Stout
Esb Red Ale

Before the invention of black patent malt, the brewers at Frederick Brewing Company believe the great London brewers made Porter like this—robust and full-bodied but not overly bitter or astringent. The round malt finish and chocolate undertones of Blue Ridge Porter will warm your body and soul. The first kegs and bottles of Blue Ridge beers rolled out in November 1993. Since then the brewery has been expanded three times.

Blue Ridge Steeple Stout

Frederick Brewing Company
103 S. Carroll St.
Frederick, MD
  21701
(301) 694-7899

Other Blue Ridge Beers:
Golden Ale
Amber Lager
Wheat Beer
Subliminator
  Dopplebock
Hopfest
Cranberry Noel
Porter
Esb Red Ale

Frederick Brewing Company's rye stout was brewed originally in 1993, in celebration of St. Patrick's Day. Today a rich, strong, black ale, Blue Ridge Steeple Stout contains more than seventy-five pounds of American grain per barrel, including barley malts, roasted barley, and rye. Almost a meal in itself, this beer is best with hearty foods, bread and cheese, and heavy desserts.

North Coast Brewing Company

455 N. Main St.
Fort Bragg, CA
 95437
(707) 964-BREW

Other Beers:

Scrimshaw Pilsner
 Style Beer
Old No. 38 Stout
Red Seal Ale

Malted wheat and the choicest American barley are combined with a blend of noble hops to create this light, fruity, refreshing beer. Brewed in the style of the American beer renaissance, Blue Star Wheat Beer is unfiltered, the yeast adding a complex note to the flavor profile. It's specially good with a slice of lemon. This beer was the winner of the 1995 silver medal at the World Beer Championships®.

Blue Suede Ale

Coophouse Brewery
2400 Industrial Ln.
  #350
Broomfield, CO 80020
(303) 466-3777

Other Beers:
Bent Lager
Liver Lager

Blue Suede Ale is Coophouse Brewery's version of an American brown ale. They encourage you to "dance the funky chicken with the Blue Suede Alien." Coophouse Brewery, in Broomfield, Colorado, has been brewing lagers and ales since March 1995. Coophouse Brewery brews in a tiny seven-barrel brewkettle, producing their righteous beer in extremely limited quantities.

Truckee Brewing Company
11401 Donner Pass Rd.
Truckee, CA 96160
(916) 587-5406

Other Beers:
Truckee Dark
Truckee Amber Lager

Truckee Brewing Company resurrected this beer to pay homage to the first California lager, which was brewed five miles east of Truckee in the town of Boca. Following the German tradition, Boca Bock is lagered for eight weeks. The result is a refined taste that you can find only in the best German beers, where time is immaterial. The most common comment: "WHOAHHHHH!!!!!"

Bohemian Pilsner

Dock Street Brewing Company

225 City Line Ave.
Suite 110
Bala Cynwyd, PA
  19004
(610) 668-1480

Other Beers:

Dock Street Amber
  Ale

Illuminator Double
  Bock

Dock Street's Bohemian Pilsner is brewed in the style of the original pilsner beers of Bohemia, in what is now the Czech Republic, in a tradition that dates to 1842. Dock Street Brewing Company uses enormous amounts of costly Czech Zatec and German Hallertau hops. Dock Street's Bohemian Pilsner is characterized by a rich, golden color and a soft, complex, malty flavor. It is balanced by a clean, gentle hop "nose" and a long, dry finish. Dock Street's Bohemian Pilsner is a voluptuous pilsner beer!

Boston Red

Boston Beer Works®
61 Brookline Ave.
Boston, MA 02215
(617) 536-BEER

Other Beers:
Fenway Pale Ale
Hercules Strong Ale
Victory Bock
Centennial Alt
Bambino Ale
Kenmore Kölsch
Beantown Nut
  Brown Ale
Buckeye Oatmeal
  Stout
Curley's Irish Stout
B.B.W. Eisbock
  Lager

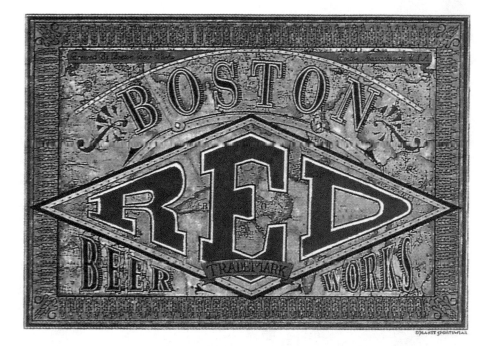

Boston Beer Works' flagship beer, first brewed on February 2, 1992, Boston Red is the beer by which all others are judged. With its deep red hue and fragrant hop aroma, this ale is a well-balanced blend of malt and hops with a refreshingly crisp, bitter finish. Brewed year-'round, Boston Red is an excellent door opener into the craft brewing revolution. Boston Beer Works is at 61 Brookline Avenue, directly across the street from historic Fenway Park, in the heart of Kenmore Square.

Boulder Fall Fest Ale

Rockies Brewing Company
2880 Wilderness Pl.
Boulder, CO 80301
(303) 444-8448

Other Boulder Beers:
Extra Pale Ale
Amber Ale
Porter
Igloo Ale
Stout
Brown Ale
E.S.B.
Singletrack
Cliffhanger

Introduced in September 1992, Boulder Fall Fest Ale is available only during the months of August, September, and October. This dry-hopped amber ale combines Mt. Hood hops with dark malt to produce a crisp finish and full aroma.

Rockies Brewing Company
2880 Wilderness Pl.
Boulder, CO 80301
(303) 444-8448

Other Boulder Beers:
Extra Pale Ale
Amber Ale
Porter
Igloo Ale
Fall Fest
Brown Ale
E.S.B.
Singletrack
Cliffhanger

Boulder Stout is a traditional stout that is handcrafted for lovers of true dark ale—robust with a hearty flavor, slight chocolate finish, and a full aroma. It was the 1994 Great American Beer Festival® silver medal winner in the stout category and a gold medal winner at the 1995 World Beer Championships®.

Boyne Beer

Boyne USA Resorts
P.O. Box 19
Boyne Falls, MI
  49713-0019
(800) GO-BOYNE

Boyne Mountain and Boyne Highlands, located in northwestern Michigan, have launched their own pilsner brew with a distinctive, rich taste. The brew is available in draft and in 12-ounce green bottles. The Boyne pilsner is produced specifically for Boyne USA Resorts under the supervision of the brewmasters at the Frankenmuth Brewery in Frankenmuth, Michigan. The refreshing pilsner is a full-bodied brew that boasts a smooth flavor. The product is sold in the resorts' dining rooms and lounges, as well as in package liquor stores and restaurants throughout Boyne Country.

Rock'n M Brewing Company
401 E. Main
Belgrade, MT
59714   (406) 388-2007

Other Beers:
Double Tree Wheat
Emigrant Red
Ballard Nut Brown
Butte Beer

BREWED & BOTTLED BY ROCK'N M BREWING CO., BELGRADE, MONTANA

ROCK'N M

M

BREWING COMPANY

BRANDING IRON BITTER

Classic Ale

Net. Wt. 12 FL. OZ. (355ml)

This yellow-labeled ale is a classic "Burton-on-Trent" English-style amber bitter. Branding Iron Bitter is a top-fermented ale with a distinctive malty full body; a robust, fruity bouquet; and a mouth-watering finish. This recipe is a second-generation ale brew. The biggest complaint about some ales is that they have too much of a hop bite. The brewers have smoothed out the bite so the drinker can enjoy the full-bodied flavor of a classic ale.

Brooklyn Lager

Brooklyn Brewery
118 N. 11th St.
Brooklyn, NY 11211
(718) 486-7422

Other Brooklyn Beers:
Brown Ale
East India Pale Ale
Black Chocolate Stout

Brooklyn Lager is a revival of Brooklyn's robust pre-Prohibition beers. It is an award-winning, crisp, amber lager that combines the traditional malty palate of the original Vienna style with the fruity, floral character of American hops. Dry-hopping accentuates fruity, floral notes in the aroma. Superior balance and smoothness make it a great beer to complement a wide range of foods.

Hudepohl-Schoenling Brewing Company
1625 Central Pkwy.
Cincinnati, OH 45214
(513) 241-4344

Other Beers:
Little Kings Cream Ale

Bruin Pale Ale is a rich, top-fermented ale brewed in the style of classic American pale ales. Bruin's search for the finest ingredients includes domestic and imported two-row pale, and chocolate malts hopped with Cascade, Mt. Hood Hallertau, and imported aromatic hops. The result is an ale of exquisite taste and deep amber color.

Bubba Dog Beer

Yellow Rose Brewing Company
17201 San Pedro Ave.
San Antonio, TX 78232
(210) 496-6669

Other Beers:

Vigilante Beer

Wildcatter's Crude
   Stout

Cactus Queen Ale

Honcho Grande
   Brown Ale

Yellow Rose Pale
   Ale

Bubba Dog Beer comes to you in limited quantities from a small South Texas brewery. It is brewed from Edwards Aquifer water, English barley malt, hops, and yeast. To ensure freshness, always keep refrigerated and consume within several weeks. Some haze or sediment may be normal in these fresh, unpasteurized, unfiltered beverages. Tastes best when enjoyed with good friends, your favorite dog, and good food!

Boulevard Brewing Company

2501 Southwest Blvd.
Kansas City, MO
  64108
(816) 474-7095

Other Boulevard Beers:

Pale Ale

Wheat Beer

Unfiltered Wheat
  Beer

Bob's '47

Irish Ale

Tenpenny American
  Bitter

Boulevard Bully! Porter is a dry, medium-bodied dark ale. Its intense dark-roasted barley malt flavor is perfectly balanced by its complex hop character. The rich flavor of Bully! Porter makes it an ideal accompaniment to a wide variety of foods. Boulevard Brewing Company, the first brewery to open in Kansas City in more than a half a century, has grown to be the largest craft/microbrewer in the Midwest.

Cactus Queen Ale

Yellow Rose Brewing Company
17201 San Pedro Ave.
San Antonio, TX
78232
(210) 496-6669

Other Beers:
Vigilante Beer
Wildcatter's Crude
   Stout
Bubba Dog Beer
Honcho Grande
   Brown Ale
Yellow Rose Pale
   Ale

Cactus Queen Ale comes to you in limited quantities from a small South Texas brewery. It is brewed from Edwards Aquifer water, English barley malt, hops, and yeast. To ensure freshness, always keep refrigerated and consume within several weeks. Some haze or sediment may be normal in these fresh, unpasteurized, unfiltered beverages. Tastes best when enjoyed with good friends and good food!

Captain Bastard's Oatmeal Stout

Squatters Brewery
375 W. 200 S.
Salt Lake City, UT
  84101
(801) 328-2329

Other Beers:
Squatters Hefeweizen
Beehive Lager
Hop Head Red

Captain Bastard's Oatmeal Stout is a wonderfully smooth and flavorful oatmeal stout brewed with oatmeal, roasted barley, pale caramel, and chocolate malts. Mt. Hood hops provide a delicate aroma. Squatters Brewery found the demand for their fine ales and lagers growing faster than their brewing capacity. So in January 1994 they purchased the historic Henderson Building to expand their production. The brewery addition, Fuggles, has the ultimate capacity to produce 30,000 barrels a year and has begun supplying its brews to clubs, restaurants, ski resorts, and hotels along the Wasatch front.

Catamount Amber

Catamount Brewing Company
58 S. Main St.
P.O. Box 457
White River Junction, VT
  05001
(802) 296-2248

Other Catamount Beers:
Gold
Porter
Pale Ale
Octoberfest
American Wheat
Bock
Christmas Ale

Catamount Amber's deep copper color and rich, full-bodied flavor are the products of North American malted barley milled at the brewery. The tart hop character comes from a blend of Perle and Willamette hops. Pure water and a select strain of top-fermenting yeast complete the list of all-natural ingredients. Catamount Brewing Company, founded in 1985, is Vermont's original microbrewery. Located in the historic railroad village of White River Junction, the brewery offers free tours and tastings.

Catamount American Wheat

Catamount Brewing Company

58 S. Main St.
P.O. Box 457
White River Junction, VT
  05001
(802) 296-2248

Other Catamount Beers:

Gold
Porter
Pale Ale
Octoberfest
Amber
Bock
Christmas Ale

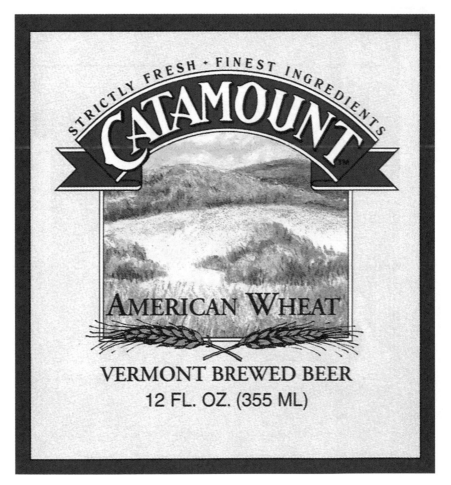

A new style in the brewing renaissance, American Wheat complements the long, lazy days of summer with its crisp, refreshing body and subtle, tart finish. Pale gold in color with a white, frothy head, it is extremely crisp and refreshing. American Wheat is slightly tart with a soft, well-rounded finish. Catamount Brewing Company, founded in 1985, is Vermont's original microbrewery. Located in the historic railroad village of White River Junction, the brewery offers free tours and tastings.

Catamount Christmas Ale

Catamount Brewing Company
58 S. Main St.
P.O. Box 457
White River Junction, VT
  05001
(802) 296-2248

Other Catamount Beers:
Gold
Porter
Pale Ale
Octoberfest
Amber
American Wheat
Bock

A classic India Pale Ale, Catamount Christmas Ale is deep red in color with a full, malty body and pronounced Cascade hop finish. It is a perfect warmer for the chills of winter. Catamount Brewing Company, founded in 1985, is Vermont's original microbrewery. Located in the historic railroad village of White River Junction, the brewery offers free tours and tastings.

Catamount Brewing Company
58 S. Main St.
P.O. Box 457
White River Junction, VT
  05001
(802) 296-2248

Other Catamount Beers:
Gold
Porter
Pale Ale
Amber
American Wheat
Bock
Christmas Ale

This full-bodied lager is brewed with North American two-row malts, giving Catamount Octoberfest a smooth malt character. This is a Vienna-style amber lager, crisp as an autumn day. It is enhanced by a mellow yet spicy hop accent. This unique balance is achieved with the addition of fresh Hallertau and Northern Brewer hops, traditionally used by German brewers. The color is a deep, rich, autumn gold, with hints of orange. Catamount Brewing Company, founded in 1985, is Vermont's original microbrewery. Located in the historic railroad village of White River Junction, the brewery offers free tours and tastings.

Cave Creek Amber Ale

Black Mountain Brewing Company
6245 E. Cave Creek Rd. Cave Creek, AZ 85331
(602) 488-6597

Other Beers:
Black Mountain Gold
Cave Creek Chili Light
Frog Light
Phoenician Premium Pilsner
Grand Canyon Premium Beer
Cave Creek Chili Beer

The Arizona desert. Home to twenty million rattlesnakes, scattered F-16 parts, and lizards the size of beagles. All baked to a crisp 130°F. It's the kind of wide-open desolation that makes people think twice before shutting off the car. And a place where a cold beer is pretty damn important. Black Mountain Brewing Company of Cave Creek, Arizona, has produced a highly drinkable, beautifully colored copper Amber Ale with the perfect blend of hops and yeast for a very smooth taste. For those who find other ambers to be too hoppy, Cave Creek will be perfect for their palates.

Cave Creek Chili Beer

Black Mountain Brewing Company

6245 E. Cave Creek Rd.
Cave Creek, AZ
   85331
(602) 488-6597

Other Beers:

Black Mountain Gold

Cave Creek Chili
   Light

Frog Light

Phoenician Premium
   Pilsner

Grand Canyon
   Premium Beer

Cave Creek Amber
   Ale

The only beer in the world with a chili pepper in every bottle! This premium all-malt pilsner beer contains no additives, no preservatives, and no adjuncts. Black Mountain Brewing Company uses only the most costly two-row malted barley; imported yeast and hops; and pure, dedicated well water. Cave Creek Chili Beer is pasteurized to ensure a long shelf life. The edible chili pepper gives this golden lager a unique and full-bodied green chili flavor and is great for cooking as well.

Centennial Alt

Boston Beer Works®
61 Brookline Ave.
Boston, MA 02215
(617) 536-BEER

Other Beers:
Fenway Pale Ale
Hercules Strong Ale
Victory Bock
Boston Red
Bambino Ale
Kenmore Kölsch
Beantown Nut
  Brown Ale
Buckeye Oatmeal
  Stout
Curley's Irish Stout
B.B.W. Eisbock
  Lager

Alt is a German word meaning "old," and Boston Beer Works' Centennial Alt is brewed in accordance with strict German traditions. Winner of the 1994 Great American Beer Festival's® silver medal in the Düsseldorf-style Altbier category, Centennial Alt is a deep amber ale with a very malty aroma and a rich, full-bodied flavor. It is brewed every 100th batch at the brewery; hence its name. Boston Beer Works is at 61 Brookline Avenue, directly across the street from historic Fenway Park, in the heart of Kenmore Square.

Shields Brewing Company
24 E. Santa Clara St.
Ventura, CA 93001
(805) 643-1807

Other Beers:
Shields Stout
Channel Islands Ale
Gold Coast Beer

Channel Islands Wheat is a light, flavorful, German-style wheat beer. Served with a slice of lemon, Channel Islands Wheat is a superb Southern California thirst quencher. Channel Islands Wheat is an award-winning beer popular among the local tourist trade and locals alike. Established in 1990, Shields Brewing Company became the first operational brewery in Ventura County since the 1800's.

Cherry Rail

Cherryland Brewery Ltd.
341 N. 3rd Ave.
Sturgeon Bay, WI
  54235
(414) 743-1945

Other Beers:
Silver Rail
Golden Rail
Door County
  Raspberry Bier
Apple Bach

Cherry Rail beer is a light-lagered fruit beer flavored with the essence of Door County cherries. A well-balanced lambic beer with just a light, subtle hint of fruit, it was awarded a silver medal in the fruit beer category at the Great American Beer Festival® in 1991. Cherryland Brewery was founded in 1987 and is located on northeastern Wisconsin's Door County Peninsula. The brewery is open year-'round for daily tours, 9:00 A.M. to 5:00 P.M.

Chickies Rock Cream Ale

Starview Brewing Company
51 Codorus Furnace Rd.
Mt. Wolf, PA 17347
(717) 266-5091

Chickies Rock Cream Ale was introduced in June 1995. It's the first beer from Starview Brewing Company. This wonderful-tasting cream ale is brewmaster Mike Knaub's rendition of what a cream ale might have been like during the mid- to late 1800s. Cream ale is an American invention that was based on the Bohemian-style pilsners that started the lager revolution. Bohemian-style pilsners were malty as well as hoppy beers compared to today's version. The hopping rate has been cut down to give Chickies Rock Cream Ale a personal touch and a delectable taste.

Chocolate Stout

Bison Brewing Company
2598 Telegraph Ave.
Berkeley, CA 94704
(510) 841-7734

In the Mayan and Aztec civilizations of Central and South America, cocoa beans were considered so precious they were used as money. On special occasions, Montezuma himself served his palace guests chocolate in goblets of beaten gold. Farther up the coast and several centuries later, Bison Brewing Company brews a richly textured stout by mashing in powdered cocoa beans along with the dark-roasted and caramelized malts. The flavor melds so completely in the stout as to be almost seamless, yet the mysterious power and richness of chocolate emerges beckoning all to raise a golden goblet (or 22-ounce bottle) to their lips. The brewery brews over 50 unique seasonal beers each year, handcrafted from fresh local ingredients.

Coho Pacific Extra Pale Ale

Bridgeport Brewing Company
1313 N.W. Marshall St.
Portland, OR 97209
(503) 241-7179

Other Beers:
Blue Heron Pale Ale

XX Stout

Pintail Extra Special Bitter

Old Knucklehead Barleywine

Bridgeport India Pale Ale

Bridgeport Porter

A traditional English-style light ale, Coho Pacific is a honey-hued and light-bodied bitter. It's delicately hopped with a combination of Nugget, Willamette, and Fuggle hops. Bridgeport ales are made with two-row malted barley from Oregon and Washington, supplemented by imported English specialty roasted barley malts. Hops from the Pacific Northwest, reputed to be some of the finest hops in the world, also are used in the brewing process. Bridgeport Brewing Company is Oregon's oldest operating microbrewery and is in Portland, a leading city in the microbrewing renaissance.

Cole Porter

SLO Brewing Company
1119 Garden St.
San Luis Obispo, CA
  93401
(805) 543-1843

Other Beers:
Brickhouse Extra
  Pale Ale
Garden Alley
  Amber Ale
Holidaze Ale

Unless you've got X-ray vision, you can't see through a glass of SLO Brewing Company's Cole Porter. And now it is available in 22-ounce "Fat Boy" bottles. Based on a traditional English-style porter made with seven different barley malts, SLO Brewing Company's version adds a unique chocolate/coffee richness to create what brewmaster and owner Michael Hoffman calls the "Schwartzenegger of our beers." Tours of the brewery are available on request.

Columbus Pale Ale

The Columbus Brewing Company
500 S. Front St.
Suite 770
Columbus, OH 43215
(614) 241-2070

The Columbus Brewing Company, in the historic Brewery District of Columbus, Ohio, has been in operation since 1988. Columbus Pale Ale has grown to be The Columbus Brewing Company's flagship brand, with a loyal Midwest following, and was named "Best Beer in Ohio" along the way. When visiting central Ohio, be sure to stop by and say hello.

Corolla Gold

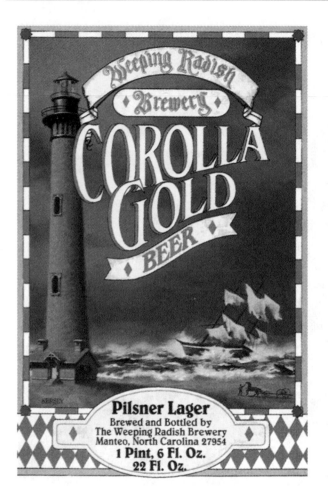

Weeping Radish Brewery
P.O. Box 1471
Manteo, NC 27954
(800) 896-5403

Other Beers:
Fest Beer

Black Radish Dark
  Lager

Double Bock
  Christmas Beer

Corolla Gold is made from all-natural ingredients—water, malted barley, hops, and yeast—in accordance with the Reinheitsgebot (Purity Law) of 1516. This beer is not pasteurized and has no chemical additives or preservatives. While this beer does not have to be refrigerated, it is best if kept cooled. With a deep, rich taste, Corolla Gold is a mid-Atlantic favorite.

Cream City Pale Ale

Lakefront Brewery, Inc.
818A E. Chambers St.
Milwaukee, WI 53212
(414) 372-8800

Other Beers:
Riverwest Stein Beer
Klisch Pilsner
East Side Dark
Lakefront Cherry Beer
Lakefront Bock Beer
Lakefront Holiday Spice

Cream City Pale Ale, a top-fermented amber-colored ale, is brewed using generous amounts of malt and kettle hops. The trademark of this ale is its beautiful hop bouquet and taste, which come from a liberal dry-hopping of the highest-grade cluster hops during the secondary fermentation. The malty firmness of this ale comes from the perfect mixture of two-row malted barley, carapils, and caramel specialty malts. The ale has an original specific gravity of 1.060 and is fermented at 65°F, which imparts the classic ale fruitiness to the brew. Since the brewery's ales are not filtered, this product can be classified as a real ale.

Cutthroat Pale Ale

NO PRESERVATIVES   ALL NATURAL

CUTTHROAT

PALE ALE

12 FL. OZ.

Uinta Brewing Company
389 W. 1700 S.
Salt Lake City, UT
  84115
(801) 467-0909

Other Beers:
King's Peak Porter
Uinta Hefe Weizen
India Pale Ale

Cutthroat Pale Ale has a rich, copper color with a clean, complex, malty fullness. It has a very slight accent on fruity, estery overtones and a dry, hoppy finish. Uinta Brewing Company's beers are brewed in European styles using only the finest basic ingredients in each batch: malted barley, hops, water, and yeast. No adjuncts or preservatives are used, and the beer is never pasteurized.

**William & Scott
Brewing Company**
2130 Main St.
Suite 250
Huntington Beach, CA
   92648
(800) 788-HORN

Other Beers:
American Amber Ale
Peach Honey Wheat
Winterful

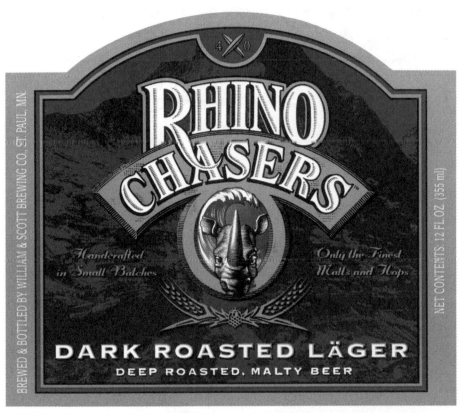

The deep-amber Dark Roasted Läger of Rhino Chasers is a handcrafted American beer brewed in the great German dark-lager tradition. Brewed with richly toasted malt and with a smooth, robust flavor, Dark Roasted Läger is a very drinkable beer. This beer was a silver medal winner in the amber lager category at the 1994 Great American Beer Festival®. If you'd like to try an award-winning Rhino Chasers ale, it's best to have it on draft. It's easy to tell which establishments carry Rhino Chasers on draft—just look for the rhino horn tap handle at a tavern near you. Rhino Chasers is not just another beer; rather, it's the ultimate microbrew experience.

Dead Horse India Pale Ale

McNeill's Brewery
90 Elliot St.
Brattleboro, VT
  05301
(802) 254-2553

Other Beers:
Oatmeal Stout
Duck's Breath Ale
Firehouse Amber Ale
Pullman's Porter
Extra Special
  Bitter Ale
Professor Brewhead's
  Brown Ale

Dead Horse India Pale Ale is handmade from the choicest English winter variety barley malt and lots of fresh whole flower hops. This brew is fully aged and never filtered. For more information about this product write McNeill's Brewery or drop by their pub, open after 4:00 P.M. daily, where you can sample beer directly from the brewery cellars.

Baltimore Brewing Company
104 Albemarle St.
Baltimore, MD 21202
(410) 837-5000

Other DeGroen's Beers:
Pils
Weizen
Maibock
Doppelbock
Weizenbock
Altfest
Märzen
Rauchbock
Helles

DeGroen's Dunkles is a clean-tasting dark lager beer with a slightly roasted aroma. A smooth, full-bodied malty beer with a subtle amount of hops, its popularity peaks during the fall and winter months. The Baltimore Brewing Company opened in 1989 and is a small but fast growing producer of fine crafted beers in the German tradition.

DeGroen's Märzen

Baltimore Brewing Company
104 Albemarle St.
Baltimore, MD 21202
(410) 837-5000

Other DeGroen's Beers:
Pils
Weizen
Maibock
Doppelbock
Weizenbock
Altfest
Dunkles
Rauchbock
Helles

DeGroen's Märzen started as a seasonal beer when it was first introduced during Oktoberfest of 1990. In 1991 the Baltimore Brewing Company decided to keep it year-'round due to its popularity. It has since developed into their largest-selling beer. Like all Märzen beers, DeGroen's is deep amber in color and is an exceptionally smooth and full-bodied lager beer.

Denali Ale

Bird Creek Brewery
310 E. 76th Ave., #B
Anchorage, AK 99518
(907) 344-2473

Other Beers:
Alaskafest Winter Ale
Anchorage Ale
Iliamna Wheat
Raspberry Wheat Beer
Old 55 Pale Ale

Denali Ale is an American-style mild brown ale made with premium Wisconsin two-row barley, roasted to a golden Alaskan sunset color, and mashed to an original gravity of 1.045. This is a malty brew balanced by a mixture of Chinook and Cascade hops for bitterness, and finished with the bouquet of wildflowers at Denali Park, the exclusive locale of these flowers. Bird Creek Brewery was founded in 1991 by brewmaster Ike Kelly, and is named after his hometown of Bird Creek, nestled on the shores of a mountain fjord south of Anchorage.

Dergy's Amber Ale

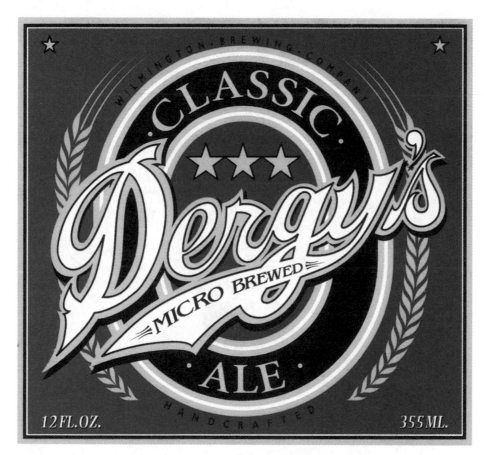

Wilmington Brewing Company
111 Bryan Rd.
Wilmington, NC
  28412
(910) 791-BEER

Other Dergy's Beers:
Golden Ale
Porter
Riverfest Ale
Winter Ale
Summer Ale

Dergy's Amber Ale, also known as a pale ale, has a slightly red hue, and a slightly nutty flavor well balanced with bold hops. Since Wilmington Brewing Company's debut in December 1994, Dergy's English-style ales have been well received; the brewery takes a lot of pride in being able to brew consistent, quality ales and is proud to brew North Carolina's premier microbrewed ales. Dergy's Amber Ale was honored as a silver medal winner in the 1996 World Beer Championships®.

Deschutes Brewery Jubelale

Deschutes Brewery
901 S.W. Simpson Ave.
Bend, OR 97702
(541) 385-8606

Other Beers:
Bachelor Bitter
Black Butte Porter
Cascade Golden Ale
Obsidian Stout

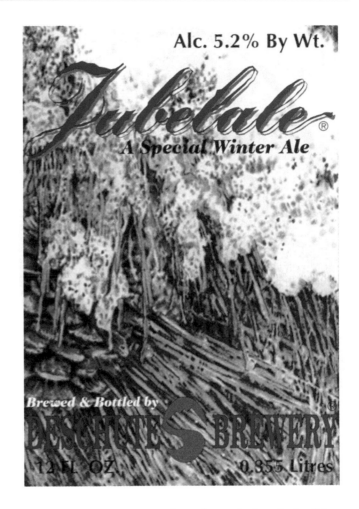

Deschutes Brewery Jubelale, rich and full-bodied, is produced each year for release during the holiday season. Enjoy this very special ale with close friends and our warmest holiday wishes. Cheers!

Desperado Special Bitter

Coast Range Brewing Company
7050 Monterey St.
Gilroy, CA 95020
(408) 842-1000

Other Beers:
Blackberry Wheat Ale
California Blonde Ale
Irish Stout
India Pale Ale
Auld Lang Syne
  Holiday Ale

This is Coast Range Brewing Company's flagship beer and one of the finest pale ales you will find. Desperado Special Bitter incorporates both British and American ale traditions. Its deep amber color and rich malt body come from domestic two-row malt and four of the finest British pale and crystal malts. A generous amount of Pacific Northwest hops supply a well-balanced bitterness and fragrant floral bouquet. Coast Range Brewing Company's proprietary strain of yeast provides a fresh, fruity aroma and a clean, satisfying finish. A complex malt profile and balanced hoppiness make Desperado Special Bitter a classic beer-drinking experience.

Door County Raspberry Bier

Cherryland Brewery Ltd.

341 N. 3rd Ave.
Sturgeon Bay, WI 54235
(414) 743-1945

Other Beers:

Silver Rail
Golden Rail
Cherry Rail
Apple Bach

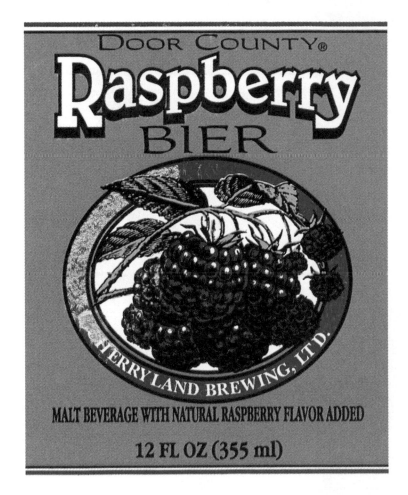

Door County Raspberry Bier is a light-lagered fruit beer flavored with the essence of Wisconsin raspberries. It has a soft, delicate bouquet of raspberry that finishes with a tart fruit flavor. Door County Raspberry Bier has been a crowd favorite at numerous beer tastings. Cherryland Brewery was founded in 1987 and is on northeastern Wisconsin's Door County Peninsula. The brewery is open year-'round for daily tours, 9:00 A.M. to 5:00 P.M.

Double Bag Ale

Long Trail Brewing Company
U.S. Rte. 4
P.O. Box 168
Bridgewater Corners, VT
  05035
(802) 672-5011

Other Long Trail Beers:
Kölsch
Brown Ale
Hibernator
India Pale Ale (I.P.A.)
Stout
Long Trail Ale

Long Trail Brewing Company's Brown Bag Ales series is a way for the brewery to offer their customers a range of beer styles that are not widely available. Several times a year, the style will change. Double Bag Ale, the brewery's third offering in the series, is a high-gravity double *Alt*, or *Stickebier*, in the tradition of the *Altbier*-producing breweries of Düsseldorf, Germany.

Lost Coast Brewery
123 W. 3rd St.
Eureka, CA 95501
(707) 445-4485

Other Beers:
Alley Cat Amber Ale

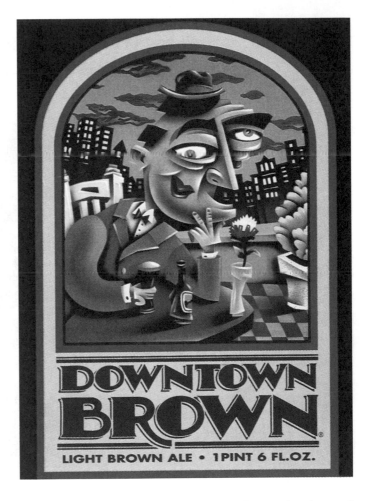

Downtown Brown is a smooth, full-bodied, nut-brown ale lightly hopped with a hint of roasted and crystal malts. This ale is dark in color without the heavy taste of a porter or stout. A superb beverage to be enjoyed with food. This award-winning ale may be enjoyed with a fine meal at the Lost Coast Brewery and Café in Eureka, California, or in the comfort of your own home.

Drayman's Porter

Berkshire Brewing Company
12 Railroad St.
South Deerfield, MA
  01373-0096
(413) 665-6600

Other Beers:
Steel Rail Extra Pale
  Ale
Berkshire Ale

Berkshire Brewing Company's Drayman's Porter is a full-bodied, dark ale with a pleasant, chocolate/roasted malt flavor. It has a slightly malty sweetness that is balanced with a delicate hop bitterness, flavor, and aroma, giving a smooth and memorable taste experience.

Dubuque Star "River Town" Brown

**Dubuque Brewing
Company**
500 E. 4th St.
Dubuque, IA
  52001-2398
(319) 583-2042

**Other Dubuque
Star Beers:**
"Big Muddy"
  Unfiltered Red Ale

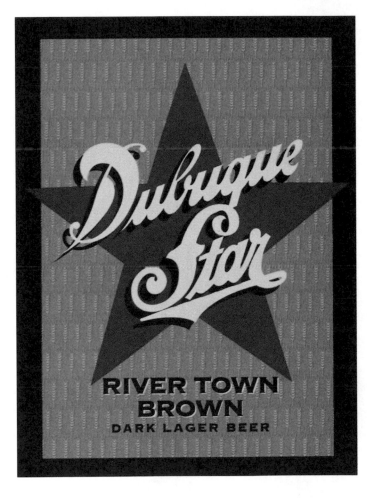

The city of Dubuque, Iowa, would certainly not have developed into one of the busiest spots in the American heartland during the early 1800s had it not been for the giant, rolling Mississippi River. Residents of river towns such as Dubuque maintain a permanent and unspoken respect for the power of its waters. Dubuque Brewing Company's dark lager beer is rich brown in color from the generous use of chocolate malt, a smooth and full-flavored brew that is lightly hopped and slightly dry on the finish.

81

Earthquake Porter

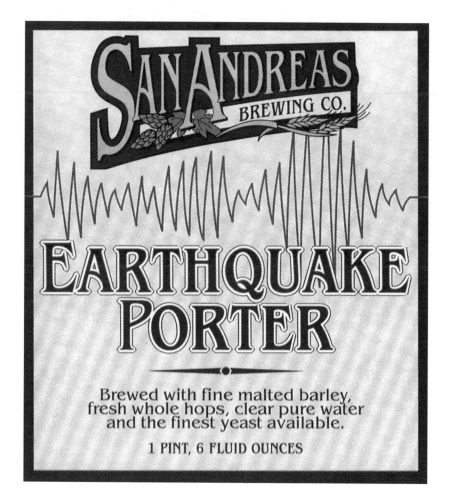

San Andreas Brewing Company
737 San Benito St.
Hollister, CA 95023
(408) 637-7074

Other Beers:
Earthquake Pale
Seismic Ale
Kit Fox Amber
Cranberry Ale
Apricot Ale
Survivor Stout

For lovers of dark beer, this full-bodied brew is just right. Earthquake Porter is made with roasted barley and pale, crystal, and chocolate malts to produce a rich, chocolate-coffee-flavored wort. Increased amounts of Cascade, Goldings, and Chinook hops, added during the kettle boil, balance out the strong malt flavors of this hearty, smooth, and satisfying porter.

Easy Street Wheat

Odell Brewing Company
800 E. Lincoln Ave.
Fort Collins, CO 80524
(970) 498-9070

Other Beers:
90 Shilling
Levity Ale

A light and refreshing ale, Easy Street Wheat gets its name from the brewers "taking it easy" by not filtering the beer. The remaining natural proteins and yeast, which are more commonly filtered out for the sake of appearance, result in a slight cloudiness. The yeast, rich in vitamin B, gives the beer a pleasant smoothness and a slightly citrus character. The brewery is proud of this beer's gold medal finish in the American wheat category at the 1993 Great American Beer Festival®.

Eddie McStiff's Raspberry Wheat

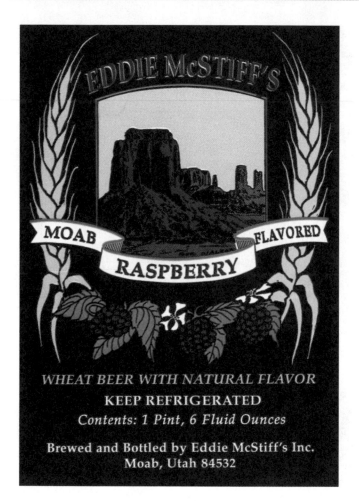

Eddie McStiff's
57 S. Main
Moab, UT 84532
(801) 259-2337

Other Beers:
Lime Ale
Jalapeno Beer
Blueberry Stout
Canyon Cream Ale
McStiff's Wheat
  Beer
McStiff's Stout
Blueberry Wheat
Arches Amber Ale
Chestnut Brown
Cherry Wheat
Spruce Beer
Orange Blossom

Eddie McStiff's Raspberry Wheat has a pleasant raspberry nose. A refreshing wheat beer and a light fruit finish have made this an award-winning brew. Naturally reduced fresh raspberries are the secret, combined with the crispness of wheat and just the right amount of hops. Even those who think it sounds terrible agree it tastes great.

The Lion Brewery, Inc.
700 N. Pennsylvania Ave.
P.O. Box GS
Wilkes-Barre, PA 18703
(800) 233-8327

Other Beers:
Stegmaier Porter
Brewery Hill Black
  & Tan
Brewery Hill Honey
  Amber Ale
Brewery Hill Raspberry
  Red Ale
Liebotschaner Cream Ale
Brewery Hill Pale Ale
Brewery Hill Cherry
  Wheat

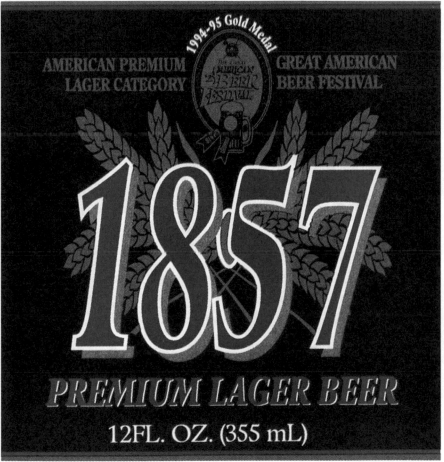

1857 Premium Lager is a superpremium, European-style lager. This all-natural brew is distinguished by its clean, full taste and rich golden color. Taste the magic of 1857 Premium Lager, a product of The Lion Brewery, Wilkes-Barre, Pennsylvania.

Elfin Ale

Star Brewing Company
5231 N.E. Martin
   Luther King, Jr., Blvd.
Portland, OR 97211
(503) 282-6003

Other Beers:
Pineapple Ale
Hop Gold Ale
India Pale Ale
Nut Brown Ale
Raspberry Wheat Ale
Altbier Ale
Black Cherry Stout

Brewed to celebrate the holidays and the winter solstice, Elfin Ale is a strong ale with a rich, chewy, chocolatey body, a luscious winter warmer without all those spices to get in the way of this classic winter style. The cognacs of the beer world, winter warmers were first brewed in England. Commonly referred to as old ale or strong ale, winter warmers may be aged up to a year or more. Elfin Ale is a celebration of barley and hops and is brewed to be shared. Elves were known to haunt wild places; so, too, does, Elfin Ale. Please drink in moderation.

Elm City Connecticut Ale

New Haven
Brewing Company
458 Grand Ave.
New Haven, CT 06513
(203) 772-BREW

Premiering in 1989, this critically acclaimed brew has been featured on tap and in bottles in virtually every location where lovers of fine traditional ales gather to imbibe. The brewery believes that there is a formula for all of this success—the wonderfully balanced flavor and smooth drinkability their product poses. When describing Elm City Connecticut Ale, critics have compared it to everything from brown ale to English mild to Scottish ale. The brewery feels that this inability to categorize their brew proves what they have been saying all along—that this is a unique product, indigenous to southern New England, one you must truly seek out and find if you want to be sure you've tasted the best that life has to offer.

87

Eureka 1881 Black & Tan

Jones Brewing Company
254 2nd St.
P.O. Box 746
Smithton, PA 15479
(412) 872-BEER

Other Eureka 1881 Beers:
Gold Light Lager
Gold Lager
Red Irish Amber

Eureka Black and Tan Welsh-style dark beer is a congenial unification of Jones Brewing Company's classic fermented lager and the brewery's noble porter, brewed with rich, aromatic hops.

Wainwright Brewing Company
3410 Sassafras St.
Pittsburgh, PA
  15201-1321
(412) 682-7400

Other J. J. Wainwright's Beers:
Evil Eye Oktoberfest
Evil Eye Honey Brown
Black Jack Black
  & Tan

Evil Eye Ale is a specialty crafted ale containing the finest hops and malts for its sparkling clarity and fine golden color. Wainwright Brewing Company, founded in 1821, merged with twenty other breweries in 1899 as part of Pittsburgh Brewing Company. The recipes used today to brew Wainwright's beers are the original recipes that have been retrieved from the archives.

Extra Special Southern Lager

Stone Mountain Brewers
3595 Canton Rd.
Suite 9A-313
Marietta, GA 30066
(404) 423-1491

Stone Mountain Extra Special Southern Lager is a unique beer that is meticulously brewed from the finest barley malt, brewing water, hops, and yeast; no cereal grains are used. By brewing this lager southern style, and in small batches, strict control is possible and an unusually superb taste with real southern drawl is achieved.

Eye Of The Hawk Select Ale

Mendocino Brewing Company
13351 Hwy. 101 S.
P.O. Box 400
Hopland, CA 95449
(707) 744-1015

Other Beers:
Blue Heron Pale Ale
Black Hawk Stout
Frolic Shipwreck Ale
Yuletide Porter
Red Tail Ale
Peregrine Pale Ale
Springtide Ale

The Eye, as it is known to its many devotees, is a strong, high-gravity, well-balanced amber ale brewed by Mendocino Brewing Company of Hopland, California. The recipe uses a large amount of pale and caramel two-row malt blended with several hop varieties. When this complex hop nature combines with the richness of the malt, the result is a smooth, robust ale characterized by a clean, crisp finish.

Fat Tire Amber Ale

New Belgium Brewing Company
500 Linden St.
Fort Collins, CO 80524
(970) 221-0524

Other Beers:
Abbey Belgian Style Ale
Sunshine Wheat Beer
Trippel Belgian Style Ale
Old Cherry Ale

Fat Tire Amber Ale is a dry-hopped, amber ale with a distinctive nutty malt flavor and a fresh, hoppy aroma. A small amount of live yeast remains in the bottle, giving the beer a freshness and fullness of character otherwise lost by sterile-filtration and pasteurizing processes. Fat Tire Amber Ale should be served cool, not cold, to best experience the rich aroma and complex flavors.

Fire Rock Pale Ale

Kona Brewing Company
75-5629 Kuakini Hwy.
Kailua-Kona, HI 96740
(808) 334-1133

Other Beers:
Pacific Golden Ale

Fire Rock Pale Ale is brewed with pale and Munich malts for a rich amber color and full flavor, then balanced with a crisp character of Galena, Cascade, and Mt. Hood hops. Kona Brewing Company produces fresh Hawaiian ale brewed with their own strain of brewer's yeast and Kona water naturally filtered through a volcanic aquifer.

Flying Fish Golden Ale

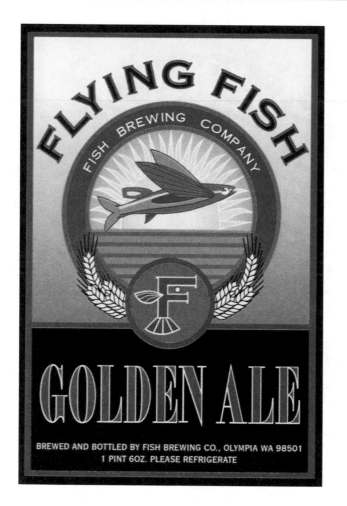

Fish Brewing Company
515 Jefferson St., S.E.
Olympia, WA 98501
(360) 943-6480

Other Beers:
50 Fathoms ESB

Fish Eye India Pale Ale

Fish Tale Pale Ale

Mudshark Dark Porter

Trout Stout

Leviathan Barley Wine

Poseidon's Old Scotch Ale

Flying Fish Golden Ale is a medium-bodied, rich golden ale with a gentle, sweet malt character. In addition to the specialty Munich and Vienna malts, the brewers have added rye malt in the amount of 10 percent of the total grist. The rye malt's spicy flavor is a perfect foil for the sweetness of the other malts. To balance the malt flavor, Flying Fish uses two new varieties of Northwest hops—Columbus for a delicate bitterness, and late kettle additions of Ultra hops, for a truly unique finish.

Founder's Stout

The Mishawaka Brewing Company
3703 N. Main St.
Mishawaka, IN 46545
(219) 256-9994

Other Beers:
INDIAna Pale Ale
Lake Effect Pale Ale
South Shore Amber Ale
Four Horsemen Ale

Founder's Stout is an Irish-style dry stout brewed with seven types of malt and three hop varieties. It has an initial malt and rich, roasted coffee flavor with a distinctively dry-roasted bitterness in the finish. This beer was a silver medal winner at the 1995 Great American Beer Festival® in the dry stouts category and a silver medal winner at the 1996 World Beer Championships®.

Four Horsemen Ale

The Mishawaka Brewing Company
3703 N. Main St.
Mishawaka, IN 46545
(219) 256-9994

Other Beers:
INDIAna Pale Ale
Lake Effect Pale Ale
South Shore Amber Ale
Founder's Stout

Four Horsemen Ale is a full-bodied ale with assertive hop qualities and a pronounced residual maltiness. It has a deep reddish-copper color and is brewed in the style of an English extra-special bitter (ESB) using five malts and three hop varieties. This beer was a silver medal winner at the 1994 Great American Beer Festival® in the traditional bitter category and a silver medal winner at the 1995 World Beer Championships®.

Frankenmuth Extra Light

Frankenmuth Brewery
425 S. Main St.
Frankenmuth, MI
  48734
(517) 652-6183

Other Frankenmuth Beers:
Weisse
Bock
Dark
Pilsener
Oktoberfest

Frankenmuth
E·X·T·R·A
Light
NATURALLY LIGHT, FIRE-BREWED BEER
12 FL. OZ. (355 ML.)
Average Analysis Per Bottle:
Calories 97, Carbohydrates 6.1 grams, Protein 1 gram, Fat 0.0 grams

Introducing a naturally light, fire-brewed beer with unsurpassed flavor and no extra calories. This American-brewed light beer is carefully crafted and brewed in small batches, with uncompromising quality by a German brewmaster. With only ninety-seven calories per 12-ounce bottle, it is truly one of the lightest beers available. Only the finest natural ingredients, expertly selected, are harmoniously blended to create this superb light beer. Frankenmuth Extra Light is brewed in the tradition of award-winning beers.

Frankenmuth Weisse

Frankenmuth Brewery
425 S. Main St.
Frankenmuth, MI
  48734
(517) 652-6183

Other Frankenmuth Beers:
Extra Light
Bock
Dark
Pilsener
Oktoberfest

Frankenmuth Weisse is a traditional Bavarian "Hefeweizen" beer in which fine bits of German yeast remain in the bottle. This refreshing Weisse beer contains only the finest, natural ingredients: more than 50 percent wheat malt, barley malt, German and American hops, pure water, and specially selected German yeast. Frankenmuth Weisse is fermented at low temperatures and aged for many weeks at near-freezing temperatures to enhance its crisp, refreshing flavor. Ideal for the warm months of the year. Enjoy the smooth, refreshing taste of Weisse!

**Frio Brewing
Company**
1905 N. St. Mary's
San Antonio, TX
  78212
(210) 225-8222

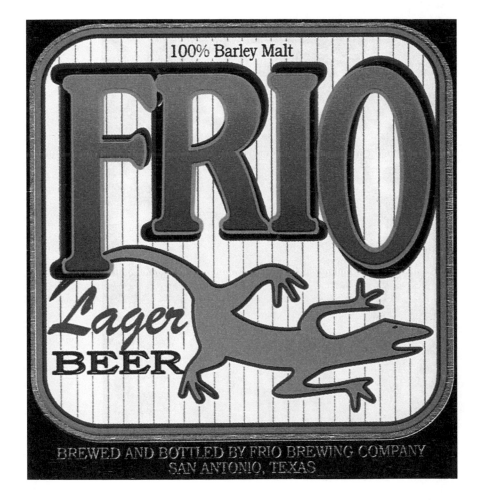

Frio Lager is brewed in small batches in Frio Brewing Company's little brewery in San Antonio, Texas. The brewery uses five different barley malts and the most aromatic hops flowers to give you a rich, fresh-tasting beer. Cold fermentation and aging give Frio Lager its clean, crisp finish.

Full Sail Amber Ale

Full Sail Brewing Company
506 Columbia St.
Hood River, OR
 97031
(503) 386-2281

Other Beers:
Full Sail Golden Ale
Full Sail Pilsner
WasSail Winter Ale

Founded in 1987, Full Sail Brewing Company is currently Oregon's largest craft brewery, with 52,000 barrels of production during 1994. Full Sail Amber Ale is the number one selling bottled craft brew in Oregon. It is a rich, nicely balanced ale with a delicate butterscotch flavor, finishing with the tang of spicy floral hops. The staff at Full Sail welcomes you to visit the brewery and taste their gorgeous brews from the Columbia River gorge!

Garten Bräu Bock

Capital Brewery Company

7734 Terrace Ave.
Middleton, WI
  53562-0185
(608) 836-7100

Other Garten Bräu Beers:

Lager
Special
Dark
Wisconsin Amber
Weizen
Maibock
Oktoberfest
Wild Rice
Winterfest
Doppelbock
The Razz
  (Raspberry Wheat)
Liam Mahoney's
  Brown Ale

Capital Brewery Company's Garten Bräu Bock is a dark, superbly flavored beer. Increased amounts of expensive specialty malts make for a beer that keeps away the winter chill! The brewery houses a unique gift shop and a laid back beer garden where the various Garten Bräu beers can be sampled.

Garten Bräu Doppelbock

Capital Brewery Company
7734 Terrace Ave.
Middleton, WI
  53562-0185
(608) 836-7100

Other Garten Bräu Beers:
Lager
Special
Dark
Wisconsin Amber
Weizen
Maibock
Oktoberfest
Wild Rice
Winterfest
The Razz
  (Raspberry Wheat)
Liam Mahoney's
  Brown Ale
Bock

A mighty beer indeed! Doppelbock is a strong bock beer—very rich, with a great depth of malt complexity. This flavor comes from the use of large amounts of specialty malts, and the beer is brewed in a fashion that concentrates these flavors. This is a very time-consuming and expensive beer to produce. Huge yet very drinkable, this malt-emphasized beer is balanced by an understated hop bittering. These flavors are most appreciated when this beer is allowed to warm up a bit. Tease yourself by enjoying the bouquet, then sip and enjoy! And please, enjoy in moderation.

Gaslight Pale Ale

Pacific Hop Exchange Brewing Company
158 Hamilton Dr. #1A
Novato, CA 94949
(415) 884-2820

Other Beers:

Grain Trader Wheat Ale

'06 Stout

Holly Hops Winter Ale

Cherry Porter

Special Brown Ale

Wheat Wine

Barbary Coast Barley Wine

India Pale Ale

Pacific Hop's biggest seller, Gaslight Pale Ale is dry-hopped for aroma with Tettnanger hops. Light caramel in color and well balanced between bitter and malt in the mouth, this ale is filtered for clarity. Just before the last of the Barbary Coast saloons was closed to make way for a fancy antique store, the brewery heard an old-timer recalling how it was at the turn of the century in that neighborhood. The story gave them the idea to name their pale ale Gaslight.

Geary's London Style Porter

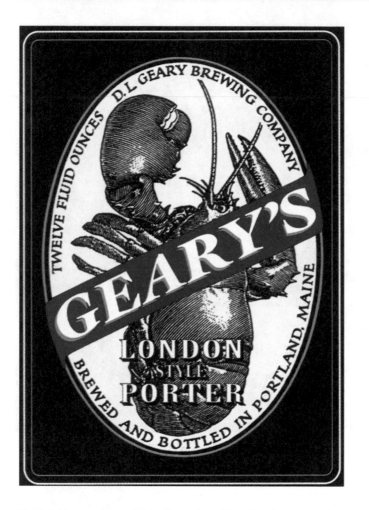

D. L. Geary Brewing Company
38 Evergreen Dr.
Portland, ME 04103
(207) 878-BEER

Other Beers:
Geary's Pale Ale
Hampshire Special Ale

Faithfully re-created by Geary's, this classic porter in the English-style porter has a deep mahogany color and a restrained, roasted-malt flavor. The result is rich and complex yet smooth and refreshing. D. L. Geary's first pints of brew were produced in the fall of 1986. Today it is recognized as a pioneer in America's brewing renaissance and a model of quality and excellence for the industry.

Georgia Peach Wheat Beer

Friends Brewing Company
P.O. Box 29464
Atlanta, GA 30359
(404) 986-8505

"The Southern Belle of Ales," Georgia Peach Wheat is a light, refreshing beer that's perfect for the beer drinker who is looking for something different, and it's the only beer in the country brewed with peaches. Georgia Peach is a wheat beer that has a splash of peach flavor. It is made with 40 percent malt barley, 40 percent malt wheat, and 20 percent peaches, with a blend of Cascade and Hallertau hops.

Goat's Breath Bock

Signature Beer Company
2737 Hereford St.
St. Louis, MO
  63139
(314) 772-5911

It's not the bottom of the barrel! Despite the familiar rumor, bock is not made by scraping the bottom of the barrel at cleaning time. Bock beer originated as a springtime beer many years ago in Germany, where *bock* means "goat." Goat's Breath Bock is brewed from real spring water. Its toastiness is derived from a blend of six different malts. Enjoy!

Gold Nectar Ale

Humboldt Brewing Company
856 10th St.
Arcata, CA 95521
(707) 826-1734

Other Beers:
Gold Rush Ale
Oatmeal Stout
Red Nectar Ale

Gold Nectar Ale, the brewery's new addition to team nectar, is a rich, deep-golden ale created with the same quality ingredients and brewing skill that produces its award-winning cousins. It has a floral, happy bouquet and bold taste that give way to a smooth finish and a sweet malt aftertaste. Carefully selected aroma hops are used in a complex recipe to produce an exciting flavor yet easy-to-drink ale.

Golden Gate Original Ale

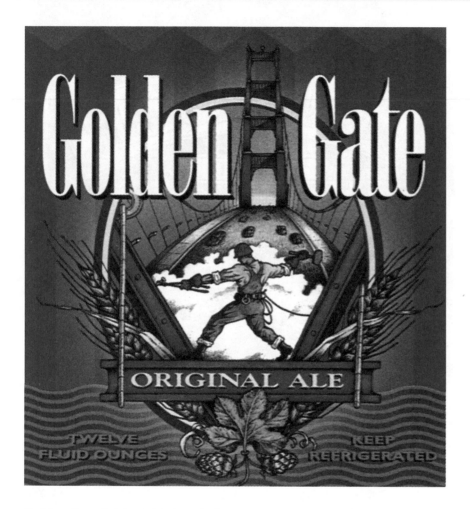

**Golden Pacific
Brewing Company**
5515 Doyle St., #4
Emeryville, CA
  94608
(510) 655-3322

Other Beers:
Hibernator Winter
  Ale
Golden Bear Lager
Black Bear Lager
Wheat Beer

Golden Gate Original Ale is a California-style copper-colored ale brewed in Emeryville with all natural ingredients, no additives, no preservatives. The malt grist is a complex blend of five different Harrington, Klages, and Munich malts, resulting in rich caramel flavors. It is hopped with five American hop varieties, which are personally selected in the field by Golden Pacific Brewing Company's brewers. The resulting hop flavors showcase Centennial and Willamette hops. The beer is bold and robust yet balanced and drinkable. It is brewed for the lover of microbrewed beer flavors.

**Riverside Brewing
Company**
1229 Columbia Ave.
Suite C4
Riverside, CA 92507
(909) 682-5465

Other Beers:
Pullman Pale Ale
Victoria Ave.
  Amber Ale
7th Street Stout
Raincross Cream Ale

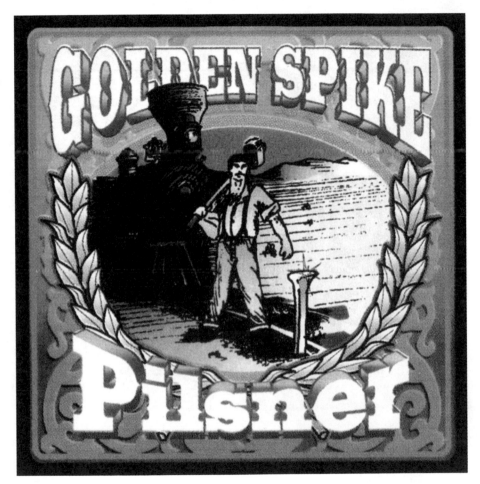

Golden Spike Pilsner is a brew laden with good body; hoppy aroma; and a big, dry, crisp Czech hop flavor. This beer has a very dry hop finish and long dry hop aftertaste, true to the classical pilsner style and very well made. The brewers at Riverside Brewing Company take great pride in the beer and produce this lager with Sazz hops.

Goose Island Christmas Ale

Goose Island Beer Company
1800 W. Fulton
Chicago, IL 60612
(312) 226-1119

Other Beers:
Kilgubbin Red Ale
Honker's Ale

Goose Island Christmas Ale is specially brewed just for the holidays. This brew is a wonderful brown ale made with Belgian specialty malts for a deep-garnet color and rich malty flavor. Crystal hops are generously added for a spicy aroma and clean finish. It is the perfect ale to toast any holiday celebration.

Goose Island Honker's Ale

Goose Island Beer Company
1800 W. Fulton
Chicago, IL 60612
(312) 226-1119

Other Beers:
Kilgubbin Red Ale
Christmas Ale

Goose Island's flagship brew, Goose Island Honker's Ale, is full of character and immensely drinkable. It is an exceptionally balanced American pale ale, featuring its spicy hop aroma from Styrian Goldings hops; a rich malt from the use of caramel and wheat malts along with roasted barley; a clean, crisp finish; and the color of a sunset.

Graffiti Wheat

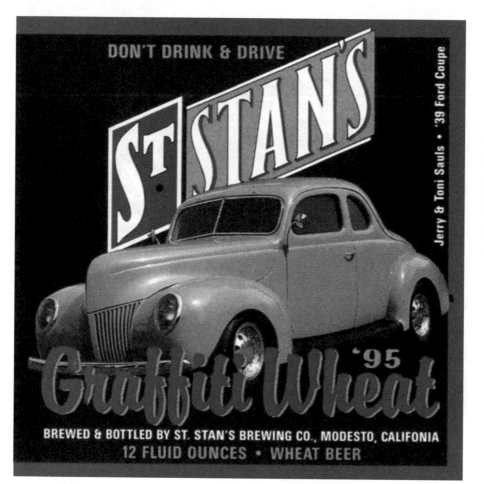

DON'T DRINK & DRIVE

ST. STAN'S

Jerry & Toni Sauls • '39 Ford Coupe

'95
Graffiti Wheat

BREWED & BOTTLED BY ST. STAN'S BREWING CO., MODESTO, CALIFONIA
12 FLUID OUNCES • WHEAT BEER

St. Stan's Brewing Company
821 L St.
Modesto, CA 95354
(209) 524-BEER

Other St. Stan's Beers:
Dark Alt
Fest Beer
Whistle Stop Pale Ale
Red Sky Ale
Amber Alt

Modesto is the hometown of film producer George Lucas. His movie *American Graffiti* was about his high school days in Modesto. Each year at the annual Graffiti festival, St. Stan's selects a "period" car from the car show that is showcased on the upcoming year's Graffiti Wheat beer label. This is the sixth series. The brewers have used a 50-50 blend of wheat malt and barley malt to produce a beer in the Bavarian Weiss tradition. The color is light and is slightly hazy. The flavor is refreshing, spicy, fruity, and, of course, wheaty. The aromatic and bittering hops are Willamette and Hallertaur.

Grant's India Pale Ale

Yakima Brewing & Malting Company
1803 Presson Pl.
Yakima, WA 98902
(509) 575-1900

Other Grant's Beers:
Scottish Ale
Imperial Stout
Celtic Ale
Weis Beer
Apple Honey Ale
Perfect Porter
Spiced Ale

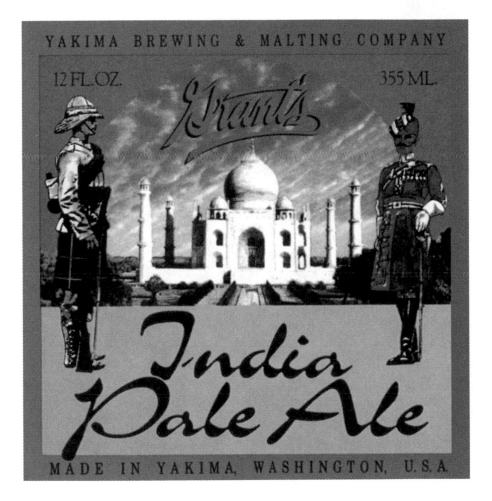

Hops were long ago found to be a good cure for beer spoilage. So when the British breweries had to send a pale ale to their troops in India in the nineteenth century, they doubled the hopping rate. Bert Grant has developed Grant's India Pale Ale, a faithful reproduction of the nineteenth-century ale. Brewed with special care, it is pale and refreshing, with a strong hoppy bitterness and aroma.

Grant's Perfect Porter

Yakima Brewing & Malting Company
1803 Presson Pl.
Yakima, WA 98902
(509) 575-1900

Other Grant's Beers:
Scottish Ale
Imperial Stout
Celtic Ale
Weis Beer
Apple Honey Ale
India Pale Ale
Spiced Ale

The history of porter is rather vague and not well documented, but based on extensive research (and his memories of Canadian porters in the 1930s and 1940s), Bert Grant has now developed Grant's Perfect Porter. Most characteristics of the older porters were derived from the brown malts used in the mashing. Grant's Perfect Porter combines the flavors of pale malt, chocolate malt, peat-smoked malt, caramel malt, and black malt with a special mashing system and a unique oak aging technique.

**Oregon Trader
Brewing Company**
P.O. Box 447
140 Hill St. N.E.
Albany, OR
  97321-0128
(541) 928-1931

Green Chili Lager is an amber lager to which Serano, Anaheim, and Hungarian Wax green chilis are added. Extra care is taken to preserve the fresh green chili flavor. This lager is cold and refreshing, followed by a pleasingly warm explosion. A true enchilada in a glass!

Gritty McDuff's Best Bitter

Gritty McDuff's
369 Fore St.
Portland, ME
  04101-4026
(207) 772-BREW

Other Beers:
Gritty McDuff's
  Best Brown

Gritty McDuff's Best Bitter begins with imported Styrian Golding hops from Slovakia, one of the finest regions in the world for growing the aromatic herb. The hops are added to the brew to balance the slight malt sweetness, giving the beer a refreshing, fruity palate. The taste will make beer lovers believe they've opened a brew pub right in their living room.

Hale's Brewing Company
4301 Leary Way N.W.
Seattle, WA 98107
(206) 706-1544

Other Beers:
Hale's Honey Wheat
Hale's Celebration
  Porter
Hale's Pale Ale
Hale's Special Bitter

First introduced on July 4, 1983, Hale's Pale Ale is the Northwest's premier pale ale. Hale's Pale Ale is a golden-colored, evenly balanced ale possessing a nutlike maltiness and a crisp, dry finish. Try it and experience an ale that helped kick-start the microbrewery revolution in the Great Northwest.

Hampshire Special Ale

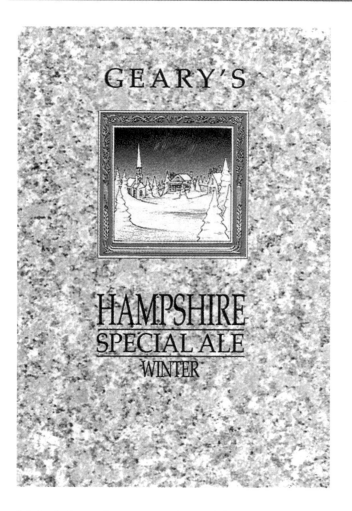

**D. L. Geary
Brewing Company**
38 Evergreen Dr.
Portland, ME 04103
(207) 878-BEER

Other Beers:
Geary's Pale Ale
Geary's London
    Style Porter

Maine's legendary seasonal specialty is available only from October to April each year. Hampshire Special Ale has a huge toasted malt flavor balanced by assertive hoppiness. The finish is long and lingering, with the malt and hop notes blending with alcohol warmth. D. L. Geary's first pints of brew were produced in the fall of 1986. Today it is recognized as a pioneer in America's brewing renaissance and a model of quality and excellence for the industry.

**Old Peconic
Brewing Company**
P.O. Box 2027
Shelter Island, NY
  11964
(516) 749-3064

Other Beers:
Hampton Ale

Hampton Gold is a delicious, well-balanced, drinkable golden ale noted for its smoothness, a result of the addition of pure clover honey at the end of the boil. When poured it offers an attractive golden color and long-lasting head. Malts include traditional two-row pale ale and Munich Lovibond. Bittering hops are Chinook and Cluster, with Kent Golding for aroma. Ale yeast is used during fermentation. Taste the true microbrew!

Hangtown Boysenberry Ale

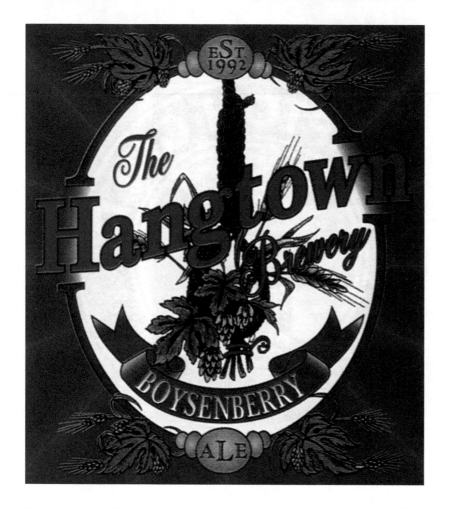

The Hangtown Brewery
560A Placerville Dr.
Placerville, CA 95667
(916) 621-3999

Other Beers:
Placerville Summer
    Ale
Stout Ale
Placerville Pale Ale

Boysenberry Ale is similar to Hangtown Brewery's Placerville Pale Ale with a fragrant boysenberry aroma. The initial taste is similar to that of Placerville Pale Ale but segues to an aftertaste that hints of fruity boysenberries. The Hangtown Brewery was started in 1989 in a 500 sq. ft. shop. Sales have since skyrocketed, thus necessitating the move to an industrial building with a storage capacity of 150 barrels.

Harpoon Ale

Mass. Bay Brewing Company
306 Northern Ave.
Boston, MA 02210
(617) 574-9551

Other Harpoon Beers:

Harpoon India
  Pale Ale

Harpoon Pilsner

Harpoon Alt

Harpoon Light

Spring/Harpoon
  Stout

Fall/Harpoon
  Octoberfest

Winter/Harpoon
  Winter Warmer

Summer/Harpoon
  Snakebite

Harpoon Ale is made by carefully combining the finest roasted malt and the freshest Cascade hops with the brewery's rare top-fermenting yeast. Harpoon Ale has a fruity aroma and a crisp, balanced finish. Harpoon brews specialty beer for the discerning consumer who is looking for the best taste. Their beer is something more than bland and common-tasting. It is for the individual who is searching for the unique.

Harpoon Light

MASS. BAY BREWING CO., INC.
BOSTON, MA

HARPOON
L I G H T ™ BEER

12 FL. OZ.

Mass. Bay Brewing Company
306 Northern Ave.
Boston, MA 02210
(617) 574-9551

Other Harpoon Beers:
Harpoon Ale
Harpoon India Pale Ale
Harpoon Pilsner
Harpoon Alt
Spring/Harpoon Stout
Fall/Harpoon Octoberfest
Winter/Harpoon Winter Warmer
Summer/Harpoon Snakebite

Harpoon Light is brewed specifically as a light beer. This all-malt light has only 105 calories, yet does not compromise on the quality of its ingredients. Finally a light beer with real beer taste. Their brewers are slaves to their art, although it would be a lie to say that it is all work and no play. You, too, can have fun at the Harpoon Brewery. Come and enjoy a brewery tour and/or seasonal event!

Haystack Black Porter

Portland Brewing Company
2730 N.W. 31st Ave.
Portland, OR 97210
(503) 226-7623

Other Beers:
Oregon Honey Beer
Wheat Berry Brew
MacTarnahan's Ale
Uncle Otto's
  Oktoberfest
Icicle Creek Winter
  Ale
Malarkey's Wild
  Irish Ale
Bavarian Style
  Weizen

Haystack Rock at Cannon Beach, Oregon, is one of the world's largest coastal monoliths, a dark and imposing landmark on the northern Oregon coast. Haystack Black Porter is a landmark beer. The dark character of rich, roasted malts is in utter harmony with hops well chosen for their flavor and aroma. "If it's too dark—you're too young."

Heartland Weiss Beer

Chicago Brewing Company
1830 N. Besly Ct.
Chicago, IL
  60622-1210
(312) 252-2739

Other Beers:
Legacy Lager
Big Shoulders Porter
Legacy Red Ale

Chicago's Heartland Weiss Beer, made after a traditional Bavarian wheat beer, was given the bronze medal for German wheat at the 1992 Great American Beer Festival®. This Bavarian style wheat beer is brewed and bottled by Chicago Brewing Company and has a creamy head; refreshing clove aroma; and light, refreshing body.

124

Heckler Bräu Doppel Bock

Heckler Brewing Company
P.O. Box 947
Tahoe City, CA 96145
(916) 583-BRÄU

Other Beers:

Heckler Bräu Oktoberfest

Heckler Bräu Hell Lager

Heckler Bräu Doppel Bock is brewed with an extra kick. This is the beer that's inspired from the Doppel Bocks brewed by Bavarian monks for sustainment during their yearly fasts. Rich and roasty flavors tinged with smokiness. Don't confuse the sweetness and smoothness of this brew with low alcohol; because this beer has a 7.2% alcohol by volume level, drink it in moderation.

Heckler Bräu Hell Lager

Heckler Brewing Company
P.O. Box 947
Tahoe City, CA 96145
(916) 583-BRÄU

Other Beers:
Heckler Bräu
  Oktoberfest
Heckler Bräu Doppel
  Bock

Hell Lager is Heckler Brewing Company's flagship beer. Creamy malt taste, the bouquet of vanilla, honey, and floral hops. The bittersweet balance of Hell Lager is for everyday drinking, from sunup to sundown (and don't let the word hell confuse you; it's German for pale). Hell Lager is 4.9% alcohol by volume.

Summit Brewing Company
2264 University Ave.
St. Paul, MN 55114
(612) 645-5029

Other Beers:
Summit Extra
  Pale Ale
Great Northern
  Porter
Summit India
  Pale Ale
Hefe Weizen
Düsseldorfer Style
  Alt Bier
Winter Ale

Brewed in the brewery's original brewing kettles from Heimertingen, Bavaria, using German lager yeast, Czechoslovakian Saaz hops, and Belgian two-row specialty malts. Heimertingen Maibock, or May Beer, is a very malty, pale bock beer—even more pale than their Summit Extra Pale Ale. This beer is available only in April and May, so don't miss it!

Hibernator Winter Ale

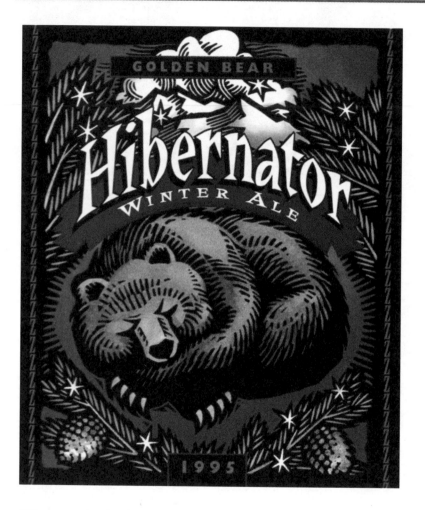

Golden Pacific Brewing Company
5515 Doyle St., #4
Emeryville, CA 94608
(510) 655-3322

Other Beers:
Golden Gate Original
   Ale
Golden Bear Lager
Black Bear Lager
Wheat Beer
Brown Ale

Hibernator is absolutely winterful. A California-style variation on a classic theme, this smooth, ruby-brown ale is Golden Pacific Brewing Company's gift to you for the holidays. Handcrafted in limited quantities, Hibernator is a velvety blend of Columbus and Kent Golding hops married with Belgian barley and mountain spring water. A little heartier, a little darker, but without the bite, Hibernator is a delightful accompaniment to holiday fare. Cozy up to one tonight.

Hickory Switch Smoked Amber Ale

Otter Creek Brewing, Inc.

85 Exchange St.
Middlebury, VT
05753
(800) 473-0727

Other Beers:

Mud Bock Spring Ale
Copper Ale
Helles Alt Beer
Stovepipe Porter
Summer Wheat Ale
Oktoberfest
Black and Tan Ale
A Winter's Ale

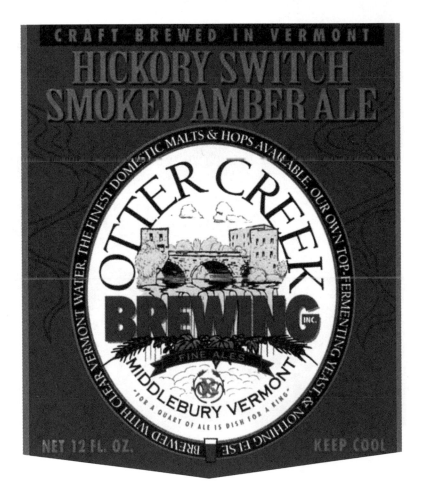

The brewery's autumn seasonal offering is Hickory Switch Smoked Amber Ale. This medium-bodied beer is brewed with a portion of malt, which is carefully smoked at Otter Creek Brewing. Its vinous notes and the dryness of the smoke perfectly complement the underlying caramel and malt flavors. Available from September to November.

129

High Rollers Wheat Beer

Anderson Valley Brewing Company

14081 Hwy. 128
P.O. Box 505
Boonville, CA 95415
(707) 895-BEER

Other Beers:

Poleeko Gold Pale Ale

Boont Amber Ale

Deep Enders Dark Porter

Belk's Extra Special Bitter Ale

Barney Flats Oatmeal Stout

Winter Solstice Select Ale

India Pale Ale

St. David's Belgian Ale

Raspberry Wheat

Millenium Ale

The High Rollers region of Yorkville, the gateway to Anderson Valley, separates and creates the valley's own pristine watershed and air basin. Like the sparkling clear water and air of Anderson Valley, High Roller Wheat sparkles with the deep golden color of the summer hills in the High Rollers region. Its dazzling head; delicate, tangy taste; and crisp, clean finish make it a summer favorite that can be enjoyed alone or with a twist of lemon. Have a Horn o' Wheat!

Highland Brewing Company

42 Biltmore Ave.
P.O. Box 2351
Asheville, NC 28802
(704) 255-8240

Other Beers:

Highland Lager

Highland Oatmeal
  Porter

Black Mocha Stout

Olde Irish Ale

Holiday Ale

Highland Celtic Ale is an English/Irish-style ale, medium amber in color with a robust, malty body and aggressively hopped. It is handcrafted with pale, crystal, and Munich malts flavored by a blend of Washington Chinook and Cascade hops. Highland's first beer, this ale is a local favorite in Asheville, North Carolina. Highland Brewing Company believes that tradition is the hallmark of excellence in brewing.

Highland Oatmeal Porter

Highland Brewing Company
42 Biltmore Ave.
P.O. Box 2351
Asheville, NC 28802
(704) 255-8240

Other Beers:
Highland Lager
Highland Celtic Ale
Black Mocha Stout
Olde Irish Ale
Holiday Ale

Highland Oatmeal Porter is very dark and malty, with a hint of mocha. This rich and flavorful beer is moderately hopped and is suited to hearty meals or after-dinner lingering. Initially produced as a seasonal beer, it has become a Highland Brewing Company staple on draft and in bottles.

Holiday Russian Imperial Stout

**Pacific Coast
Brewing Company**
906 Washington St.
Oakland, CA 94607
(510) 836-BREW

Other Beers:
Killer Whale Stout
Belgian Triple
Blue Christmas Ale
Blue Whale Ale
Columbus IPA
Gray Whale Ale

The stout of Russian czars! Brewed strong—8 percent alcohol—to withstand the long trip to Moscow from Great Britain. Black, full-bodied, and very warming. Silver medal-winning strong ale at the 1992 and 1993 Great American Beer Festival®. Pacific Coast Brewing Company has won at least one medal at that festival every year since 1988. This gives the company the longest continuing winning streak at the Great American Beer Festival® of any microbrewery its size in the nation.

Holidaze Ale

SLO Brewing Company
1119 Garden St.
San Luis Obispo, CA
   93401
(805) 543-1843

Other Beers:
Brickhouse Extra
   Pale Ale
Garden Alley
   Amber Ale
Cole Porter

Holidaze Ale is a smooth, full-bodied ale that's mellow-brewed and perfect for the winter months (it's available September through December). Its unique blend of specially roasted malts, generous array of hops, plus herbs from the mountains of Hawaii gives Holidaze Ale its rich flavor and unique aroma. Tours of the brewery are available on request.

Holy Grail Nut Brown Ale

Oldenberg Brewing Company
400 Buttermilk Pike
Fort Mitchell, KY
  41017
(606) 341-7223

Other Beers:
Premium Verum
Outrageous Bock

Holy Grail Nut Brown Ale is a very popular offering now made on a year-'round basis. The brewers at Oldenberg Brewing Company use a very rare variety of malted barley for the nutty malt flavor necessary to produce a classic in this style. The Oldenberg Brewery, five miles south of Cincinnati, in Fort Mitchell, Kentucky, is home of the American Museum of Brewing History and Arts.

Honcho Grande Brown Ale

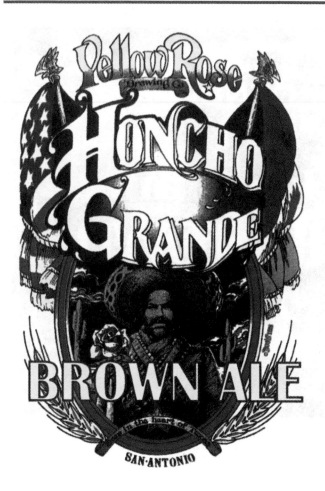

Yellow Rose Brewing Company
17201 San Pedro Ave.
San Antonio, TX 78232
(210) 496-6669

Other Beers:
Vigilante Beer
Wildcatter's Crude
  Stout
Bubba Dog Beer
Cactus Queen Ale
Yellow Rose Pale
  Ale

Honcho Grande Brown Ale comes to you in limited quantities from a small south Texas brewery. It is brewed from Edwards Aquifer water, English barley malt, hops, and yeast. To ensure freshness, always keep refrigerated and consume within several weeks. Some haze or sediment may be normal in these fresh, unpasteurized, unfiltered beverages. Honcho Grande Brown Ale won a silver medal in the 1996 World Beers Championships®. Tastes best when enjoyed with good friends and good food!

Honey Raspberry Ale

**Spanish Peaks
Brewing Company**

120 N. 19th Ave.
P.O. Box 3644
Bozeman, MT
  59772
(406) 585-0798

Other Beers:

Sweetwater Wheat
  Ale
Black Dog Ale
Yellowstone Pale Ale

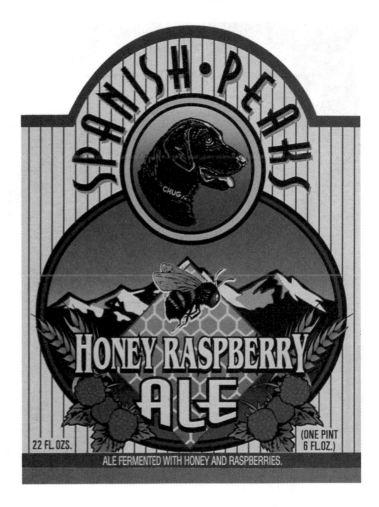

Honey Raspberry Ale was a bronze medal winner in the specialty beer category at the Great American Beer Festival® in Denver, Colorado, in 1993. It is a light-bodied amber ale made with wildflower honey and an all-natural raspberry concentrate. These ingredients, combined with five domestic and imported malted barleys, Pacific northwest Hops, water, and ale yeast, create a unique, fruity ale with a soft palate and a touch of sweetness.

Hop Gold Ale

Star Brewing Company
5231 N.E. Martin
   Luther King, Jr., Blvd.
Portland, OR 97211
(503) 282-6003

Other Beers:
Elfin Ale
Pineapple Ale
India Pale Ale
Nut Brown Ale
Raspberry Wheat Ale
Altbier Ale
Black Cherry Stout

In 1894 Louis Gerlinger built a small brewery in Vancouver, Washington. Louis named his brewery Star and began producing his world-acclaimed Hop Gold Ale. For five decades the Hop Gold Ale name was synonymous with quality. However, in 1956 the Gerlinger family sold the brewery. Star Brewing Company resurrected the Hop Gold Ale name in honor of Louis and his pioneering spirit in the Northwest beer industry. Golden in color, Hop Gold Ale has a clean, hoppy finish. A true session beer, refreshing, smooth, and low in alcohol.

Squatters Brewery
375 W. 200 S.
Salt Lake City, UT
  84101
(801) 328-2329

Other Beers:
Squatters
  Hefeweizen
Beehive Lager
Captain Bastard's
  Oatmeal Stout

Hop Head Red is a classic red ale, medium-bodied with fuggle, and with American Northwest hops providing a pleasant bitterness and fine aroma. Squatters Brewery found the demand for their fine ales and lagers growing faster than their brewing capacity. So in January 1994 they purchased the historic Henderson Building to expand their production. The brewery addition, Fuggles, has the ultimate capacity to produce 30,000 barrels a year and has begun supplying its brews to clubs, restaurants, ski resorts, and hotels along the Wasatch front.

Huckleberry Ale

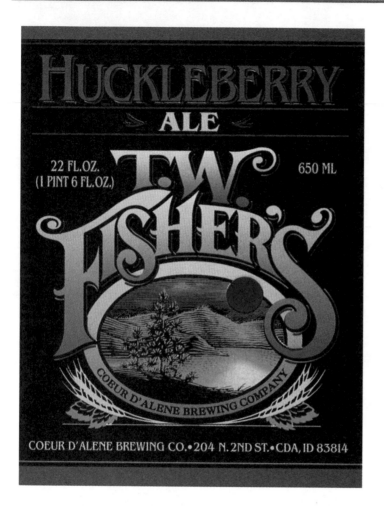

Coeur d'Alene Brewing Company
204 N. 2nd St.
Coeur d'Alene, ID
  83814
(208) 664-BREW

Other Beers:
Festival Dark Ale
Centennial Pale Ale
Cherry Porter
Red Oktober
Cream Ale
Light Wheat Beer
Ram's Head Spring
  Bock

Coeur d'Alene Brewing Company is proud to offer a taste of the best North Idaho has to offer: Huckleberries! This beer is brewed with an intoxicating hint of huckleberries, pale malt, and mild Willamette hops. Smooth, sweet, and undoubtedly refreshing!! The brewery produces only a limited amount of its exclusive beer with extremely rigid quality standards.

Woodstock Brewing Company
P.O. Box 1000W
20 St. James St.
Kingston, NY 12401
(914) 331-2810

Other Beers:
St. James Ale
Big Indian Porter
Ichabod Crane
   Holiday Lager

Hudson Lager is made with Catskill Mountain water, freshly ground malted barley, select fresh hops, and a pure strain of Bavarian lager yeast. It is not pasteurized and does not contain any additives or preservatives. This is "beer at its best." Woodstock Brewing Company is in the historic city of Kingston, on the banks of the Hudson River at the foot of the Catskill Mountains. A century ago, between New York City and Albany, there were twenty-two breweries along the Hudson, and Kingston was home to several of them. By the early 1940s the last one had closed.

Hunterbräu Amber Lager

Randy's Fun Hunter Brewery
841 E. Milwaukee St.
Whitewater, WI 53190
(414) 473-8000

This amber beer is a full-flavored, malty lager that is the flagship beer for Randy's Fun Hunter Brewery, which opened in January 1994 and is in Whitewater, in the southeastern part of Wisconsin. Hunterbräu Amber Lager remains Randy's top-selling brew.

Illuminator Double Bock

**Dock Street
Brewing Company**
225 City Line Ave.
Suite 110
Bala Cynwyd, PA
   19004
(610) 668-1480

Other Beers:
Dock Street Amber
   Ale
Bohemian Pilsner

Dock Street's Illuminator Double Bock is handcrafted from the finest barley malt, fresh German Tettnang, and Hallertau hops. It is distinguished by its full, round, malty palate, complemented by tangy, dry-hop overtones with a dense, rocky head and fresh, spicy hop "nose." Most double bock beers have names that end in "ator," in homage to the first revered bock beer, from Paulaner, "Salvator."

Independence Ale

Independence Brewing Company
1000 E. Comly St.
Philadelphia, PA
  19149
(215) 537-BEER

Other Beers:
Independence Gold
Independence Lager

Independence Ale is a pale ale with both English and American influences. It is light amber in color due to the recipe's specialty malts. Made from two-row malt and four specialty malts, plus a touch of wheat and three varieties of hops, this beer has a full-bodied and hoppy flavor with a dry, nutty finish. Independence Brewing Company welcomes you to visit their 32,000-square-foot brewery in Northeast Philadelphia. Independence Brewing Company's beers are a distinct departure from mass-produced national and pseudomicrobrands devoid of character.

**The Mishawaka
Brewing Company**
3703 N. Main St.
Mishawaka, IN
  46545
(219) 256-9994

Other Beers:
Lake Effect Pale Ale
South Shore Amber
  Ale
Four Horsemen Ale
Founder's Stout

INDIAna Pale Ale is brewed true to style of an India pale ale (IPA), with relatively high alcohol content and high hop bitterness. Aggressively hopped with Target Wye, Cascades, Centennial, and Cascade hops. Dry-hopping gives INDIAna Pale Ale a strong floral aroma with a strong hop taste in the beginning, a slightly malty middle, and a lingering bitterness in the finish.

Ipswich Ale

Ipswich Brewing Company
23 Hayward St.
Ipswich, MA 01938
(508) 356-3329

Other Beers:
Ipswich Dark Ale
Ipswich Oatmeal
   Stout

Handcrafted from the finest hops, barley and ale yeast by the Ipswich Brewing Co. Ltd., Ipswich, *Ale* Massachusetts.

Pale in color with a bold taste, Ipswich Ale is here! Not since the merchant ships regularly sailed into Ipswich Bay has Boston's North Shore known a brew like this. Ipswich Ale is Ipswich Brewing Company's flagship product. Ipswich Ale is handcrafted from the finest hops and barley malt and naturally conditioned. It's an original recipe that's unfiltered for purity and unbeatable for taste. Sail into the experience!

Boulevard Brewing Company

2501 Southwest Blvd.
Kansas City, MO
64108
(816) 474-7095

Other Boulevard Beers:

Pale Ale

Wheat Beer

Unfiltered Wheat Beer

Bob's '47

Tenpenny American Bitter

Bully! Porter

Boulevard Irish Ale, Boulevard Brewing Company's springtime seasonal beer, is patterned after red ales that have a rich Irish heritage. The recipe combines five kinds of malt to provide a complex, toasty flavor and reddish hue. Chinook and English Kent Golding hops are added to enhance the beer's complexity and to produce a pleasing balance. Boulevard Brewing Company prides itself as Missouri's second-largest brewery.

Iron Horse Dark Ale

Lonetree Brewing Ltd.
375 E. 55th Ave.
Denver, CO 80216
(303) 297-3832

Other Beers:
Sunset Red Ale
Country Cream Ale
Snow Dog Ale
Raspberry Whacker
    Wheat Beer
Lazy Lizard Wheat
    Beer
Almond Brothers
    Amber Ale
Stone Cold Golden Ale
High Point E.S.B.
Horizon Honey Ale
Atlantis Ancient
    Whale Ale
II Angels Chili Breeze
    Ale

The use of five different grains and two select hops gives Lonetree Brewing's Iron Horse Dark Ale its smooth, rich, full-bodied flavor. Perhaps you'll detect a hint of coffee aroma or the mild, nutty flavor created from the use of roasted barley and chocolate malts. This beer is loved by many who say they don't like dark beer.

148

Maritime Pacific Brewing Company

1514 N.W. Leary Way
P.O. Box 17812
Seattle, WA 98107
(206) 782-6181

Other Beers:

Flagship Red Ale

Nightwatch Ale

Jolly Roger Christmas Ale

Clipper Gold Wheat Ale

Salmon Bay Bitter

12 FL. OZ. (354 ML.)

KEEP COLD

ISLANDER PALE

MARITIME PACIFIC

BREWING CO

PALE ALE

PALE ALE

"Brewed in the Northwest with Imagination"

BREWED BY MARITIME PACIFIC BREWING CO. SEATTLE, WA

With its light, malty flavor and subtle hop character, Maritime Pacific Brewing Company's Islander Pale Ale is a refreshingly different style of pale ale. The unique hop flavor and mild bitterness are achieved by an unusual combination of English and Czechoslovakian hops. Together with a blend of light malted barley and wheat, the unique hopping makes this ale a pleasant twist on a typical style. Try Islander Pale Ale, the "untypical" pale.

Jack Rabbit Pale Ale

Pikes Peak Brewery
2547 Weston Rd.
Colorado Springs, CO
  80910
(719) 391-8866

Pikes Peak Brewery, one of Colorado's smallest breweries, is in Colorado Springs. Jack Rabbit is truly an American beer, made with U.S. barley malt, northwestern hops, ale yeast, and Colorado mountain water. Jack Rabbit is a hoppy pale ale, with the pun fully intended.

Jamaica Red Ale

Mad River Brewing Company
P.O. Box 767
Blue Lake, CA 95525
(707) 668-4151

Other Beers:
Steelhead Extra Pale Ale
Steelhead Extra Stout
John Barleycorn
  Barleywine Style Ale

Mad River Brewing Company's Jamaica Red Ale is a full-bodied, distinctly hopped red ale with great balance and a crisp finish. Look for Steelhead ales in bottles or on draught at select locations. Kegs and case sales are available at the brewery's retail sales office in Blue Lake, California.

Jet City Rocket Red Ale

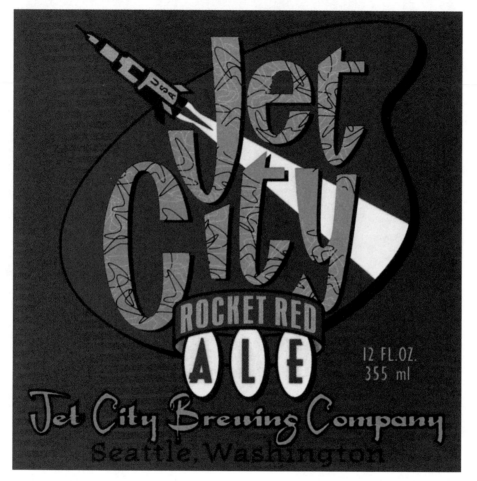

**Jet City Brewing
Company**
P.O. Box 3554
Seattle, WA 98124
(206) 392-5991

Other Beers:
Jet City Pale Ale
Jet City Triple 7
  Nectar

Jet City Rocket Red Ale is a medium- to heavy-bodied ale that has a distinctive deep red color and noticeable hoppy aftertaste. Rocket Red gets its deep red color from roasted caramel malted barley. A touch of chocolate and black patent malts also are used. A generous portion of pure Tettnang hops are added three different times in the brewing process. This brew is for the hop enthusiast.

Johnson's Authentic Amber Ale

Johnson Beer Company
2210 S. Blvd.
Charlotte, NC 28203
(704) 339-0340

Johnson's Authentic Amber Ale, a medium-bodied amber ale, uses two-row pale malt from Shreir and small amounts of English crystal for color. Hops are Chinook for a mild bitterness and Perle for aroma. This ale is dry-hopped with Willamettes for added hop character. This is an honest amber ale. Enjoy it with friends. Johnson Beer Company, a new microbrewery in a retrofitted textile mill, is just outside the city of Charlotte.

Jolly Roger Christmas Ale

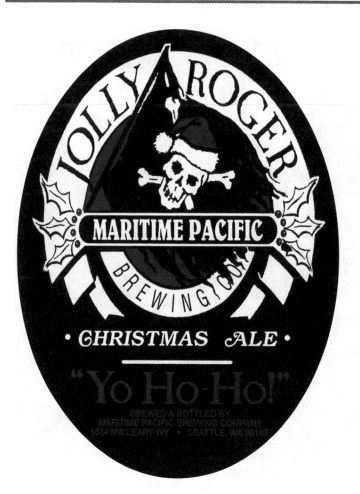

Maritime Pacific Brewing Company
1514 N.W. Leary Way
P.O. Box 17812
Seattle, WA 98107
(206) 782-6181

Other Beers:
Flagship Red Ale
Nightwatch Ale
Islander Pale Ale
Clipper Gold Wheat
  Ale
Salmon Bay Bitter

The most prized of Maritime Pacific Brewing Company's seasonal beers, Jolly Roger Christmas Ale is a truly original holiday brew, combining rich malt character with a blend of fresh Northwest Chinook and Cascade hops. The official insignia for this English-style strong ale is a smiling skull and crossbones on a black pirate flag. This emblem serves as a reminder that, like the buccaneer rogues (or "rogers") of the 1700s for whom the flag was named, this brew has been known to "keelhaul" the individual who abuses it! So enjoy your holidays with discretion, and hoist a pint of Jolly at your favorite drinking establishment. Join Maritime's salute to the era of the high-seas renegade! "Yo-ho-ho!"

Left Hand Brewing Company
1265 Boston Ave.
Longmont, CO
  80501
(303) 772-0258

Other Beers:
Sawtooth Ale

Motherlode Golden
  Ale

Black Jack Porter

Jackman's American
  Pale Ale

Maid Marion
  Berry Ale

XXXmas Ale

Imperial Stout

Juju Ginger Ale is a pale ale brewed with freshly ground ginger root. The beer is light in body, has a distinct ginger aroma, and has a very crisp finish. Left Hand Brewing Company opened in January 1994. Their capacity is 8,000 barrels per year. Left Hand Brewing Company brews only the finest beer possible (it's their life). The brewery is on the banks of the mighty St. Vrain River.

Katahdin Golden Beer

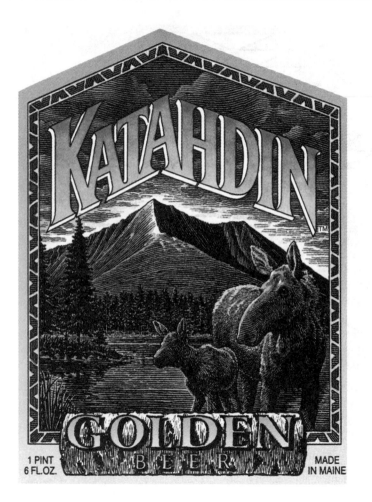

Casco Bay Brewing Company
57 Industrial Way
Portland, ME 04103
(207) 797-2020

Other Katahdin Beers:
Red Ale
Stout
Spiced Brew

Katahdin Golden Beer has a complex, distinctive flavor that is clean and crisp. The beer is cold-lagered for two weeks after fermentation to produce its smooth, clean, crisp taste. The beer is light in color and body, with a distinctive golden color. The beer is positioned as the fresh, locally brewed alternative to imported beers, hence its slogan, "The Import Alternative."

Katy Trail Pale Ale

Flat Branch Brewing Company
115 S. 5th St.
Columbia, MO 65201
(573) 499-0400

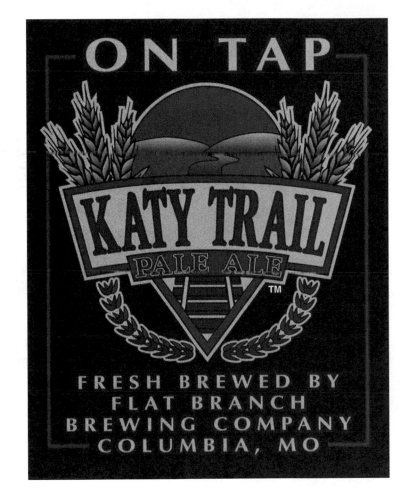

Flat Branch Brewing Company opened its doors on April 18, 1994, in downtown Columbia, Missouri. Its Katy Trail Pale Ale was inspired by the spirit of Missouri's Katy Trail recreation path. The rich amber color comes from a special combination of roasted caramel and pale malts. Combining this with rich hops, water, and ale yeast results in a natural full-bodied flavor.

157

Killer Bee Honey Ale

Hubcap Brewery
P.O. Box 3333
Vail, CO 81658
(970) 476-5757

Other Beers:
Vail Pale Ale

Guided by ancient sixteenth-century brewing methods, Hubcap Brewery bottles fewer than 600 barrels of these limited-production handcrafted ales annually. Artisan brewers carefully perfect each recipe, using only the freshest and finest barley, hops, yeast, and pure Vail water. Reminiscent of an extra-dry champagne in its lightly carbonated, medium-sweet mead, Killer Bee Honey Ale is brewed with the federally required amounts of malt and hops, and massive amounts of Colorado alfalfa honey. Enjoy!

**Pacific Coast
Brewing Company**
906 Washington St.
Oakland, CA 94607
(510) 836-BREW

Other Beers:
Belgian Triple
Blue Christmas Ale
Blue Whale Ale
Columbus IPA
Gray Whale Ale
Holiday Russian
    Imperial Stout

Killer Whale Stout is a dark, rich, roasty, smooth, and hoppy ale. It was 1990 silver medal winner and 1991 honorable mention in the stout category at the Great American Beer Festival®. Pacific Coast Brewing Company has won at least one medal at that festival every year since 1988. This gives the company the longest continuing winning streak at the Great American Beer Festival® of any microbrewery its size in the nation.

King's Pale Ale

King Brewing Company
895 Oakland Ave.
Pontiac, MI 48340
(810) 745-5900

Other Beers:
Pontiac Porter
Royal Amber Ale
Crown Brown Ale
King's Cherry Ale
King's Two Fisted
    Old Ale

King Brewing Company, in Pontiac, Michigan, is driven by the goal of bringing a variety of fresh local beer to the metropolitan Detroit area. The beer is always fresh, always traditional, and always natural. It's a simple concept: Provide a good variety of fresh local beer; no gimmicks, just good beer from an independent brewery. When in the area, stop and visit the hospitality room and taste all of the beers.

Kosmos Reserve Lager

Spoetzl Brewery
14800 San Pedro, #310
San Antonio, TX 78232
(210) 490-9128

Other Beers:
Shiner Bock Beer

Kosmos Reserve Lager was named after the brewery's first brewmaster, Kosmos Spoetzl, a Bavarian brewmaster who came to Shiner, Texas, in the early 1900s. Kosmos is a 100 percent malt brew with a unique blend of body, flavor, and up-front character. Spoetzl Brewery in Shiner, Texas, is the oldest independent brewery in the state and has been handcrafting exceptional beers since 1909.

Lazy Lizard Wheat Beer

Lonetree Brewing Ltd.
375 E. 55th Ave.
Denver, CO 80216
(303) 297-3832

Other Beers:
Sunset Red Ale
Country Cream Ale
Iron Horse Dark Ale
Snow Dog Ale
Raspberry Whacker
    Wheat Beer
Almond Brothers
    Amber Ale
Stone Cold Golden Ale
High Point E.S.B.
Horizon Honey Ale
Atlantis Ancient
    Whale Ale
II Angels Chili Breeze
    Ale

Kick back, relax, and enjoy a cold, tasty brew with a lively new taste. Besides quality barley, hops, and malted wheat, a bit of pure lime extract has been added to Lazy Lizard Wheat Beer. To really excite those taste buds, enjoy this beer from a cold, salt-rimmed glass with a slice of lime. Created exclusively for Pine Street Brewing Compnay, it's a taste sensation that lounge lizards love.

Chicago Brewing Company
1830 N. Besly Ct.
Chicago, IL
  60622-1210
(312) 252-2739

Other Beers:
Big Shoulders Porter
Heartland Weiss Beer
Legacy Red Ale

Chicago's Legacy Lager, formulated to re-create the rich, full-flavored beer produced prior to Prohibition, is the first beer ever to win back-to-back European pilsner gold medals at the 1991 and 1992 Great American Beer Festival®. This world-class beer is brewed and bottled by Chicago Brewing Company and has a fresh hop aroma; smooth malt taste; and crisp, fresh finish.

163

Legacy Red Ale

Chicago Brewing Company

1830 N. Besly Ct.
Chicago, IL
  60622-1210
(312) 252-2739

Other Beers:

Legacy Lager

Big Shoulders Porter

Heartland Weiss
  Beer

Chicago's Legacy Red Ale, brewed in the technique of the Celtic brewers of Ireland, was judged the top Irish ale in an international tasting of Irish beers. This delicious ale is brewed and bottled by Chicago Brewing Company and has a fresh hop aroma; rich malt body; and clean, dry finish.

Lift Bridge India Pale Ale

Lift Bridge Brewing Company
P.O. Box 2856
Ashtabula, OH
  44005-2856
(216) 964-6200

Other Beers:
Amber Lager
Oktoberfest
Winter Gale Ale
Oatmeal Stout
Eisbock

Lift Bridge India Pale Ale is a medium-bodied ale brewed in the tradition that has made it the much-sought-after style worldwide. The brewery dry-hops this ale to provide you with the fragrance and spicy finish that hop enthusiasts enjoy. This extra hop addition and generous bittering hops during boil were made famous when the English needed to transport the ale to colonial India.

Lighthouse Amber

**Santa Cruz
Brewing Company**
516 Front St.
Santa Cruz, CA
  95060
(408) 429-8838

Other Beers:
Pacific Porter
Lighthouse Lager
Beacon Barley Wine
Scott's Big Wheat
Amber Plus F.G.S.
Rye Not
Pacific Stout
Hoppy Holidays

Lighthouse Amber is Santa Cruz Brewing Company's amber-colored lager brewed from pale malted barley, caramel malt, northern brewer hops, Chinook hops, Hallertau hops, Tettnanger hops, water, and lager yeast.

Star Union Brewing Company

P.O. Box 282
Hennepin, IL 61327
(815) 925-7400

Other Beers:

Starved Rock
Amber Ale

The mythical yet legendary Honest Abe Flowenstein came to the state of Illinois with the intention of splitting a few dozen rails and constructing a small office in which he planned to practice law. However, after working in the Illinois heat and humidity for only a few hours, Flowenstein decided that he and all the thirsty pioneers arriving by the thousands needed a refreshing deep-cooper ale, aggressively hopped in small batches out of natural ingredients, to quench their thirst. As you know, the rest is history! Flowenstein's now-famous slogan can be seen and heard even today all across the Prairie State: "Thinkin' about drinkin' a Lincoln!"

Little Kings Cream Ale

Hudepohl-Schoenling Brewing Company
1625 Central Pkwy.
Cincinnati, OH 45214
(513) 241-4344

Other Beers:
Bruin Pale Ale

A first-class example of a uniquely American brewing style, Little Kings Cream Ale is substantially heavier in body and fuller in flavor than the vast majority of domestic lagers. Winner of three consecutive gold medals (in 1987, 1988, and 1989) at the Great American Beer Festival® in the American lager/cream ale category, Little Kings Cream Ale is available in 7-ounce, 12-ounce, 22-ounce, and 40-ounce bottles and draft.

Coophouse Brewery
2400 Industrial Ln.
  #350
Broomfield, CO 80020
(303) 466-3777

Other Beers:
Bent Lager
Blue Suede Ale

Liver Lager derives its name from the Irish phrase for dying of cirrhosis of the liver. After you drink too many of these pilsner-style lagers, people will be saying "the poor soul got a touch of the liver." Coophouse Brewery, located in Broomfield, Colorado, has been brewing lagers and ales since March 1995. Coophouse Brewery brews in a tiny seven-barrel brewkettle, producing their righteous beer in extremely limited quantities.

Lompoc's Ginger Wheat

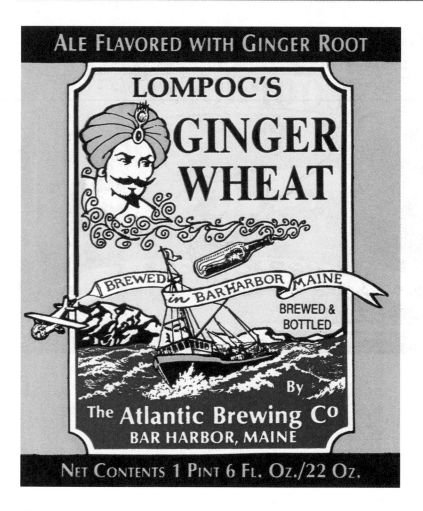

The Atlantic Brewing Company
30 Rodick St.
Bar Harbor, ME
  04609-1868
(207) 288-9513

Other Beers:
Bar Harbor
  Blueberry Ale
Coal Porter

The Atlantic Brewing Company in Bar Harbor, Maine, is proud to present Lompoc's Ginger Wheat to beer enthusiasts of New England. A light-bodied barley and wheat beer spiced with fresh ginger root to give it a refreshing taste, it is a perfect summertime brew. Contact the brewery if you are interested in a tour of their facilities.

Irons Brewing Company
2027 W. Colfax Ave.
Denver, CO 80204
(303) 985-BEER

Other Beers:
Winter Iron Winter
  Brew
Ironheart Red Ale
Dark Iron Chocolate
  Brown Ale
American Iron
  Amber Ale

This gold medal winner is brewed in the centuries-old tradition of Bohemian Pilsners. Long Iron is an assertively hopped, richly malted, pale-blond lager. Enjoy the complex blend of creamy malt body and crisp hop finish. This beer is best served at 50° F.

Long Trail Ale

12 FL. OZ. (355 ml.)

Long Trail Brewing Company
U.S. Rte. 4
P.O. Box 168
Bridgewater Corners, VT
  05035
(802) 672-5011

Other Long Trail Beers:
Kölsch
Brown Ale
Hibernator
India Pale Ale (I.P.A.)
Stout
Double Bag Ale

Long Trail Ale is Vermont's largest selling amber. Long Trail Brewing Company's flagship brew is a full-bodied, complex ale with subtle hop bitterness and is a descendant of Düsseldorf, Germany's, amber *Altbiers*. Top-fermenting yeast and cold finishing temperature result in a clean, full flavor. The brewery features a visitors' center, which is open daily for sales and complimentary tastings.

Portland Brewing Company
2730 N.W. 31st Ave.
Portland, OR 97210
(503) 226-7623

Other Beers:
Oregon Honey Beer
Wheat Berry Brew
Haystack Black
   Porter
Uncle Otto's
   Oktoberfest
Icicle Creek Winter
   Ale
Malarkey's Wild
   Irish Ale
Bavarian Style
   Weizen

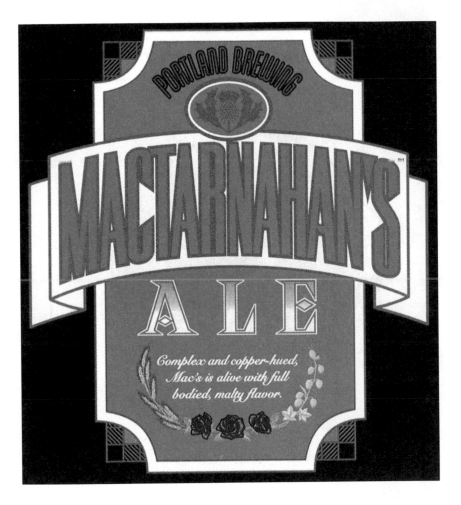

This beer was awarded a gold medal in the American pale/amber ale category at the 1992 Great American Beer Festival®. MacTarnahan's Ale is a complex, copper-colored Scottish-style ale of great character made with pale and caramel malts and Cascade hops. Scottish ales are generally heavier and stronger than their English counterparts, and this beer fits that profile. "It's hard to beat a MacTarnahan's."

Mad Anthony's Red Ale

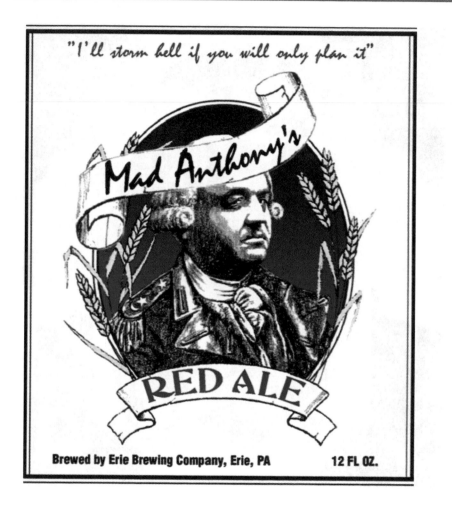

"I'll storm hell if you will only plan it"

Mad Anthony's

RED ALE

Brewed by Erie Brewing Company, Erie, PA   12 FL OZ.

Erie Brewing Company
128 W. 14th St.
Erie, PA 16501
(814) 452-2787

Erie Brewing Company has been brewing since October 1994. Mad Anthony's Red Ale is a medium-bodied red ale with a rich amber and mild sweetness. The brewery is in Erie, Pennsylvania, in historic Union Station, a restored train station from the late 1920s. Erie Brewing Company operates Hoppers Brewpub, which is open to the public seven days a week.

**Magic Hat Brewing
Company**
180 Flynn Ave.
Burlington, VT 05401
(802) 658-BREW

Other Beers:
Blind Faith
#9

The company's flagship product, Magic Hat Ale is an Irish-style red ale deep ruby-red in color with a fresh, hop nose, a big, smooth, malty flavor, and a spicy finish. To get the complexity of flavors, Magic Hat Brewing Company uses five types of malt, four varieties of hops, and a 150-year-old strain of English yeast. At Magic Hat Brewing Company ancient alchemy meets modern-day science to produce the best-tasting beer on the planet.

Mallard Bay Red Ale

Hops and Barley Beer Corporation
3440 Page St.
San Diego, CA
 92115
(619) 286-0115

Mallard Bay Red Ale is a classic red ale, with slow-roasted malty flavors, dark-copper color, and a distinctive sprucy aroma. Hops and Barley Beer Corporation traditionally brews Mallard Bay Red Ale in small batches to ensure the beer's superior quality, aroma, and taste.

Manitou Brand Amber Ale

Traverse Brewing Company Ltd.
11550 U.S. 31 S.
P.O. Box 158
Williamsburg, MI 49690
(616) 264-9343

Other Beers:
Old Mission
   Lighthouse Ale

Manitou Brand Amber Ale is an English-style ale with a deep amber color. It is well-balanced, smooth, and full-flavored, with a hint of nuttiness from the English grains used in the recipe. Four varieties of Yakima Valley hops, plus Yorkshire stone yeast give Manitou Brand Amber Ale its distinct English flavor.

Millstream Lager Beer

Millstream Brewing Company
P.O. Box 284
Amana, IA 52203
(319) 622-3672

Other Beers:
Millstream Wheat
  Beer
Schild Brau Amber

Millstream Lager is a Münchener Helles beer, with German lager yeast, six-row barley, and the finest American hops. Well-aged for robust body and a creamy head, Millstream Lager is a delight to the senses, imparting an arousing aroma and a satisfying flavor. This is a beer to discover, to enjoy, and to share with friends, a brew to savor with good company, to be consumed by itself or with your favorite foods.

Moose Juice Stout

Otto Brothers'
Brewing Company
P.O. Box 4177
Jackson, WY 83001
(307) 733-9000

Other Beers:
Teton Ale
Old Faithful Ale
Huckleberry Wheat
White Water Wheat
Teton Pass Porter

Moose Juice Stout is brewed with dark roasted malts, including chocolate malt, which makes this dry stout an especially smooth and light "user-friendly" beer. Chinook and Cascade hops offset the sweetness of the rich, dark malts and add a dryness that gives this beer palate appeal and a full, lip-smacking finish. It's the beer a moose would drink on a bitter cold winter night . . . if a moose drank beer.

Moss Bay Amber

Hale's Brewing Company
4301 Leary Way
N.W. Seattle, WA
  98107
(206) 706-1544

Other Beers:
Moss Bay Stout
Moss Bay Extra

Hale's Moss Bay Amber is an approachable, easy-drinking "session beer." It has a mellow hop character, and use of caramel and Carastan malts gives the beer its smooth malt quality. Moss Bay Amber is an excellent beer to enjoy with your meal.

Mt. Tam Pale Ale

Marin Brewing Company
1809 Larkspur
    Landing Circle
Larkspur, CA 94939
(415) 461-4677

Other Beers:
Marin Weiss

Marin Hefe Wiess

Blueberry Ale

Raspberry Ale

Albion Amber Ale

San Quentin's
    Breakout Stout

Pt. Reyes Porter

Old Dipsea
    Barleywine

Marin Doppel
    Weizen

Stinson Beach Peach

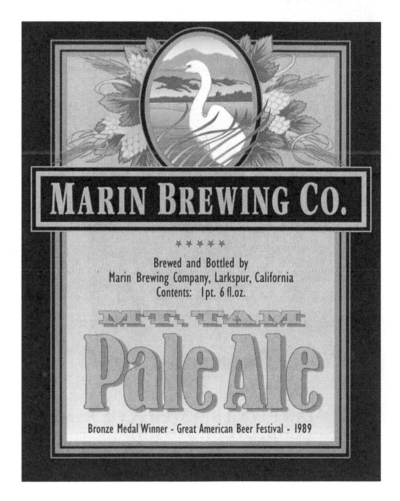

Mt. Tam Pale Ale has a bright golden color, a medium body, and a smooth taste. It is brewed with pale, wheat, and Carestan malts and combined with Cascade and Chinook hops to give it the perfect balance of flavors. This beer was also a bronze medal winner in the pale ale category in the 1989 Great American Beer Festival®.

Mount Vernon Porter

POTOMAC RIVER BREWING COMPANY
CHANTILLY, VIRGINIA

12 FL. OZ

**Potomac River
Brewing Company**
14141-A Parke Long Ct.
Chantilly, VA 22021
(703) 631-5430

Other Beers:
Patowmack Ale
Rappahannock Red Ale

Mount Vernon Porter is brewed in the traditional style favored by many of our Colonial-era brewers. The use of roasted malt gives it a robust body and deep mahogany color. The flavor profile is complex, with mild chocolate overtones and a smooth, hopped finish. Potomac River Brewing Company is a micro-brewery producing beer in small batches using only the finest ingredients available. They brew and bottle locally at their small brewery in Chantilly, Fairfax County, Virginia. Because they are a small brewery and not a beer factory, they can devote all of their time to provide a fresh, high-quality, great-tasting line of beers for you to enjoy.

Mt. Wilson Wheat Beer

Crown City Brewery

300 S. Raymond Ave.
Pasadena, CA 91105
(818) 577-5548

Other Beers:

Arroyo Amber Ale

Black Cloud Oatmeal
Stout

Yorkshire Porter

Dragon Anniversary
Ale

Oom Pah Pah
Oktoberfest

Black Forest
Dunkelweizen

Doo Dah Apan-Ale

Father Christmas
Wassail Ale

Irish Ale

Black Rose Irish Stout

Black Bear Stout

Midsummer's Night
Stout

Spring Is Here Bock

Mt. Wilson Wheat Beer is a golden American wheat-style beer with a clean finish that is perfect for the arid climate of Southern California. Inspired by the German Weiss beers, Mt. Wilson Wheat Beer is a *krystal Weissen* (clear wheat beer) produced with 25 percent malted wheat and 75 percent two-row malted barley. Cluster and Cascade hops from the Pacific Northwest are responsible for the well-balanced hop aroma. Mt. Wilson Wheat Beer proves that it is possible to have a beer that is light in color with a refreshing, full taste.

Mud Bock Spring Ale

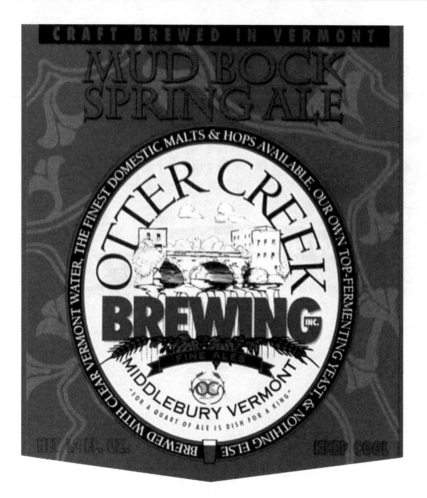

Otter Creek Brewing, Inc.

85 Exchange St.
Middlebury, VT 05753
(800) 473-0727

Other Beers:

Hickory Switch
  Smoked Amber Ale
Copper Ale
Helles Alt Beer
Stovepipe Porter
Summer Wheat Ale
Oktoberfest
Black and Tan Ale
A Winter's Ale

Mud Bock Spring Ale makes its appearance with the spring thaw. The main feature of this full-bodied beer is a broad and deep malt flavor. While sweeter than Otter Creek Brewing's other beers, a winelike character provides balance in the flavor profile. With fruity, herbal, and floral notes in the aroma, this beer celebrates the arrival of spring. Available from March to May.

Mystic Seaport Pale Ale

Shipyard Brewing Company
86 Newbury St.
Portland, ME 04101
(800) 273-9253

Other Beers:
Goat Island Light Ale
Blue Fin Stout
Old Thumper
Shipyard Export Ale
Shipyard Brown Ale
Chamberlain Pale Ale
Longfellow Winter Ale
Prelude Ale
Longfellow India
    Pale Ale
Sirius Summer
    Wheat Ale

From Mystic Seaport, The Museum of America and the Sea (Connecticut), and Shipyard Brewing Company comes an original taste of our nation's maritime past. The classic English style of Mystic Seaport Pale Ale is enhanced by its golden copper hue and creamy white head. It is dry and crisp up front with an aromatic, hoppy finish, a fitting tribute to a great American institution. Shipyard Brewing Company uses only the finest all-natural ingredients in their ales, because they are committed to brewing the freshest, most flavorful, and full-bodied ales available. Enjoy with their best wishes!

Napa Valley Red Ale

Napa Valley Ale Works
P.O. Box 5268
Napa, CA 94581
(707) 257-8381

Other Beers:
Napa Valley Wheat Ale

A full-flavored ale with only malted hops, barley, and top-fermenting yeast. No additives or adjuncts are present. Napa Valley Red Ale is not pasteurized. This allows retention of its unique flavor profile and long finish on the palate. Napa Valley Red Ale is excellent with robust foods of Latin or Mediterranean origins.

**New Amsterdam®
Company**

P.O. Box 1064
Old Chelsea Station
New York, NY
  10113-0905
(212) 473-1900

**Other New
Amsterdam® Beers:**

New York Amber
  Beer
Black & Tan
Blonde Lager
Light Amber Beer
Winter Anniversary
New York Ale

Top-fermented with an ale yeast, New Amsterdam I.D.A. has strong malt overtones with chocolate and coffee highlights in the flavor. It is produced with black malt, chocolate malt, and Victory malt, a special malt that contributes to the beer's smoothness. Northern brewer hops impart a wonderful nose to the product, which is also brewed with Willamette hops.

New York Ale

**New Amsterdam®
Company**
P.O. Box 1064
Old Chelsea Station
New York, NY
  10113-0905
(212) 473-1900

**Other New
Amsterdam® Beers:**
New York Amber
  Beer
Black & Tan
Blonde Lager
Light Amber Beer
Winter Anniversary
I.D.A.

New Amsterdam New York Ale blends American originality with the finest Old World craftsmanship. Their master brewer achieves the uniquely rich taste of New Amsterdam New York Ale through a painstaking and expensive process called "dry-hopping." Fresh, whole Cascade hop flowers are added and allowed to impart their aromatic flavor and mellow bitterness. This age-old tradition of dry-hopping is nearly extinct in this age of mass-produced beer. At New Amsterdam they know that it is the only way to brew an ale that meets their high standards.

New York Harbor Amber Ale

Old World Brewing Company
2070 Victory Blvd.
Suite 4
Staten Island, NY 10314
(718) 370-0551

Other Beers.

New York Harbor
  Dark Ale

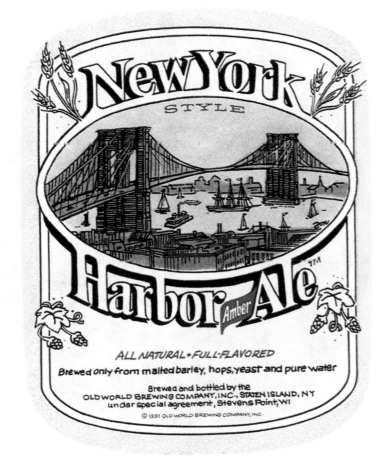

New York Harbor Amber Ale is a rich, full-bodied, robust amber ale made with 100 percent American-malted barleys: pale, caramel, Munich, and carapils. The hops are also 100 percent American. The brewers use Chinook for bittering the flavoring, and the aroma is a blend of Hallertau and Cascade. The ale is fermented for ten days, then aged an additional twenty one days. No chemicals or preservatives are used. President Sal Pennachio's dedication and passion have led the way for his beer to find its way from his basement kitchen to beer-loving consumers.

#9

not quite Pale Ale

3/4 pint

Magic Hat Brewing Company
180 Flynn Ave.
Burlington, VT
05401
(802) 658-BREW

Other Beers:
Blind Faith
Magic Hat Ale

A sort of dry, crisp, fruity, blondish, refreshing, not quite pale ale is a way of describing #9. But it's hard to describe because there's really nothing else quite like it. Magic Hat Brewing Company uses three types of malt, three varieties of hops, and a 150-year-old strain of English yeast. At Magic Hat Brewing Company ancient alchemy meets modern-day science to produce the best-tasting beer on the planet.

Nor'Wester Best Bitter Ale

**Nor'Wester
Brewery**
66 S.E. Morrison St.
Portland, OR 97214
(800) 472-BREW

**Other Nor'Wester
Beers:**
Hefe Weizen
Raspberry Weizen
Blacksmith Porter
Dunkel Weizen
Honey Weizen
Winter Weizen

Nor'Wester Best Bitter Ale is the traditional British pint of choice. Nor'Wester combines four types of pale and roasted malts, then spices the brew with more than one pound of fresh, whole flower hops per barrel to give it its characteristic spank of bitterness and aroma. This beer is top-fermented and cool-conditioned, creating a mature flavor with a balance of maltiness and hoppiness.

Nor'Wester Dunkel Weizen

**Nor'Wester
Brewery**
66 S.E. Morrison St.
Portland, OR 97214
(800) 472-BREW

**Other Nor'Wester
Beers:**
Hefe Weizen
Raspberry Weizen
Blacksmith Porter
Best Bitter Ale
Honey Weizen
Winter Weizen

Dunkel Weizen is German for "dark wheat," and Nor'Wester Dunkel Weizen is a darker version of Nor'Wester Brewery's popular Hefe Weizen. The darker color comes from two kinds of dark roasted malts added to the wheat malt grist. The resulting chocolate and coffee like flavors combined with the lighter-bodied characteristic of wheat beer give Nor'Wester Dunkel Weizen a flavor unlike a typical ale or dark lager beer.

Nutfield Old Man Ale

**Old Nutfield
Brewing Company**
22 Manchester Rd.
Derry, NH 03038
(603) 434-9678

Other Beers:
Nutfield Auburn Ale

In April 1719, a small group of families left the port city of Derry (now Londonderry), Ireland, and settled just a "barrel's roll" from this microbrewery in what was then known as Nutfield Colony. In tribute to their pioneering spirit and in recognition of the Granite State's oldest resident, the Old Man of the Mountain, Nutfield Brewing Company is proud to introduce its second beer: Nutfield Old Man Ale, a golden pale ale meticulously brewed with only the finest all-natural ingredients Mother Nature can provide. Sit back and honor the Granite State's oldest and most distinguished resident with a pint of Nutfield Old Man Ale.

O'Brien's Texas Stout

Yegua Creek Brewing Company
2920 N. Henderson Ave.
Dallas, TX 75206
(214) 824-BREW

Other Beers:
Tucker's Golden Wheat
Lucky Lady Lager
Xit Pilsner
Ice Haus Pale Ale
White Rock Red
Big D ESB
Sara's Brown Ale

O'Brien's Texas Stout is a very flavorful, black, rich, fulfilling brew. Roasted barley, oatmeal flakes, and bitter hops combine to make a great brew. Yegua Creek Brewing Company is housed in a seventy-year-old icehouse near downtown Dallas.

Old Brown Dog Ale

**Smuttynose
Brewing Company**
225 Heritage Ave.
Portsmouth, NH
  03801
(603) 436-4026

Other Beers:
Shoals Pale Ale

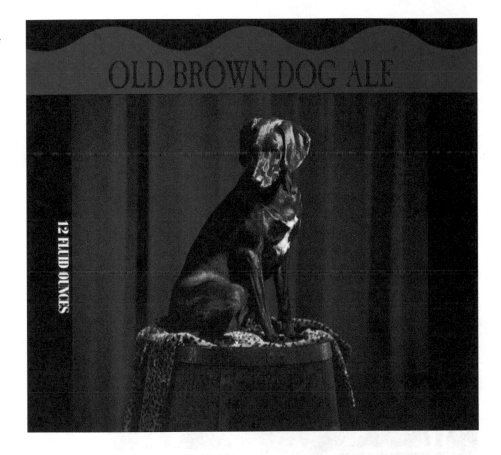

Smuttynose Brewing Company is named for Smuttynose Island, part of a small, rugged archipelago that lies off the coast of New Hampshire. Smuttynose Brewing Company brews its ales by hand, using time-honored methods and the finest ingredients, right in the seacoast city of Portsmouth, New Hampshire. Before 1995, Old Brown Dog Ale was available on draft only. This legendary brown ale, winner of a silver medal in the brown ales category at the 1989 Great American Beer Festival®, is robust, full-bodied, and bottled so you can enjoy its rich, full flavor anytime. Don't settle for just any beer. Next time tell the bartender, "Make mine a Smutty!"

Old Detroit Amber Ale

Frankenmuth Brewery
425 S. Main St.
Frankenmuth, MI
 48734
(517) 652-6183

Other Beers:
Old Detroit Red
 Lager

Frankenmuth Brewery firmly believes that the single most important attribute a beer can possess is full-bodied flavor. That's why Old Detroit Amber Ale is brewed using traditional methods, with pride in American craftsmanship and dedication to uncompromising quality. Old Detroit Amber Ale is brewed in small batches with a deep respect for the art of brewing, using only pure water, premium two-row malted barley, American hops, and specially selected strains of yeast to create its distinctive, complex flavor.

Old East India Pale Ale

Sea Dog Brewing Company
26 Front St.
Bangor, ME 04401
(207) 947-8004

Other Beers:
Old Gollywobbler Brown Ale
Windjammer Blonde Ale

Sea Dog Brewing Company has fashioned an ale after the famous ales from Burton-on-Trent that took on such bold character after surviving the long, rolling voyage in oak casts from London to Calcutta in the days of the empire. Old East India Pale Ale is truly a tawny gold masterpiece in the world of beer styles.

Old Faithful Ale

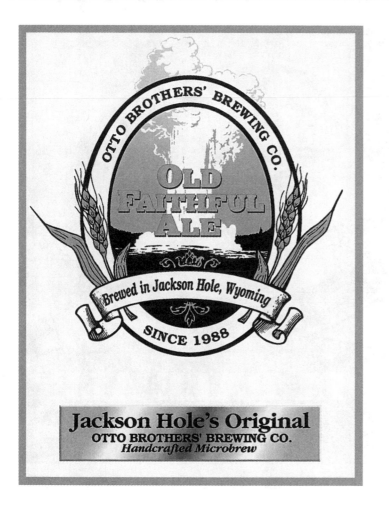

**Otto Brothers'
Brewing Company**
P.O. Box 4177
Jackson, WY 83001
(307) 733-9000

Other Beers:
Teton Ale
Moose Juice Stout
Huckleberry Wheat
White Water Wheat
Teton Pass Porter

Old Faithful Ale is named after the magnificent geyser that erupts regularly in Yellowstone National Park. The brewers at Otto Brothers' Brewing Company brew Old Faithful Ale in an American pale ale style with a special blend of Cascade and Willamette hops. These hops beautifully balance the 100 percent barley malt and provide their own memorable character to the flavor of this light golden ale. Add a gusher of excitement to your life and pop the top on an Old Faithful Ale today!

Bird Creek Brewery
310 E. 76th Ave., #B
Anchorage, AK 99518
(907) 344-2473

Other Beers:
Alaskafest Winter Ale
Anchorage Ale
Iliamna Wheat
Raspberry Wheat Beer
Denali Ale

A classic English-style pale ale, Old 55 Pale Ale is named after the year of brewmaster Ike Kelly's birth. A mixture of Wisconsin two- and six-row barley is mashed to an original gravity, then with a small percentage of caramel malt boiled with premium, Pacific Northwest Chinook and Cascade hops, Old 55 is fermented in traditional flat English fermenters before being either bottle- or cask-conditioned. This amber, smooth, full-bodied brew goes well with fireplaces, campfires, and sunsets. Bird Creek Brewery was founded in 1991 by brewmaster Ike Kelly and is named after his hometown of Bird Creek, nestled on the shores of a mountain fjord south of Anchorage.

Old Hardhead

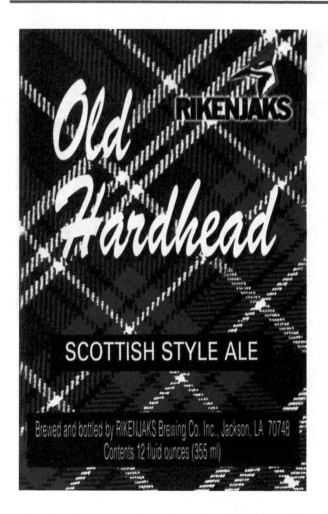

Rikenjaks Brewing Company
P.O. Box 53528
Lafayette, LA 70505
(318) 233-2802

Other Beers:
American Ale
Rikenjaks E.S.B.

Old Hardhead is a Scottish-style ale. It is medium-bodied and dark with a rich, creamy head and an accent on maltiness. Rikenjaks Brewing Company recommends that it be enjoyed as an accompaniment to hearty foods. At Rikenjaks a great deal of attention is paid to the details of brewing fine beer. It is this special commitment that makes each of their products a classic example of its respective beer style.

**Shipyard Brewing
Company**
86 Newbury St.
Portland, ME 04101
(800) 273-9253

Other Beers:
Goat Island Light Ale
Blue Fin Stout
Shipyard Export Ale
Shipyard Brown Ale
Chamberlain Pale Ale
Longfellow Winter
  Ale
Mystic Seaport
  Pale Ale
Prelude Ale
Longfellow India
  Pale Ale
Sirius Summer
  Wheat Ale

Ruled the 1988 English Supreme Champion beer, Old Thumper is an untraditional English bitter, now exclusively brewed and sold in the United States by Shipyard Brewing Company. It has hints of sweetness with apple and fruit aromas, a deceptively smooth texture, and a long, dry, hoppy finish. Shipyard Brewing Company uses only the finest all-natural ingredients in their ales, because they are committed to brewing the freshest, most flavorful, and full-bodied ales available. Enjoy with their best wishes!

201

Olde Red Eye Red Ale

Southern California Brewing Company
833 W. Torrance Blvd.
Suite 4
Torrance, CA 90502
(310) 329-8881

Other Beers:
Screaming Lobster
   Lager
California Light
   Blonde Lager
Honey Wheat Ale
Bear Country Heife
   Weizen
Buck Horn Bock
Winter Wonder

The renaissance of craft brewing in the United States started in California. The innovators of this region have developed brand-new brewing styles, and one of the most interesting is the California Red Ale. This style is set apart from the traditional English bitter style by a well-balanced caramel character, a striking ruby red visage, and a generous dosage of fresh domestic hops. Southern California Brewing Company's Olde Red Eye Red Ale is a fine example of this ale being balanced in both sweet/dry and malt/hop respects and would appeal to the beer drinker who enjoys a full-flavored ale.

Oliver Irish Red Ale

Oliver Breweries
206 W. Pratt St.
Baltimore, MD 21201
(401) 244-8900

Oliver Breweries brews traditional English ales at their Wharf Rat Pub in downtown Baltimore. Four naturally conditioned ales dispensed by hand pump and firkin and six to eight other-style ales are on offer at all times. Their popular Oliver Irish Red Ale may also be found in fine restaurants and pubs around town, including Oriole Park at Camden Yards.

Onalaska Ale

Onalaska Brewing Company
248 Burchett Rd.
Onalaska, WA 98570
(360) 978-4ALE

Other Beers:
Howlin Stout

Onalaska Ale is a smooth, well-balanced ale with nutty undertones and a slightly fruity nose. It appeals to those who prefer a very quaffable but less assertive beer. The brewers at Onalaska use three types of malt—pale two-row, Munich, and caramel—and two types of whole hop flowers—Northwest-grown Cascade and Hallertauer. This was Onalaska's first beer and still is a favorite among their long-term friends.

Rogue Ales
3135 S.E. Ferry Slip Rd.
Newport, OR 97365
(541) 867-3660

Other Beers:
American Amber Ale
Santa's Private Reserve
Rogue Ale
Cran-n-Cherry Ale
Hazelnut Brown Nectar
Mocha Porter
Rogue-n-Berry Ale
Shakespeare Stout
St. Rogue Red Ale
Dead Guy Ale
Rogue Smoke
Mexicali Rougue Ale
McRogue Scotch Ale
Old Crustacean
    Barleywine
Smoke Ale

This delicately smooth brew is deep golden in color with a rich, malty aroma and a herbal hop finish. It is made with Harrington, Klages, and Munich malts and Willamette and Cascade hops. Handcrafted in thirty-barrel batches by renowned brewer John Maier, Oregon Golden Ale derives its complex flavor from the finest hops and malts available. Like all Rogue Ales, it is made from natural ingredients with no chemical additives or preservatives.

Oregon Original India Pale Ale

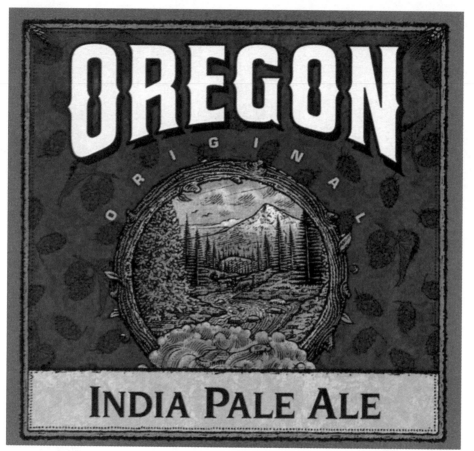

Oregon Ale and Beer Company
5875 S.W. Lakeview Blvd.
Lake Oswego, OR 97035
(503) 968-7706

Other Oregon Original Beers:
Nut Brown Ale
Hefeweizen
Raspberry Wheat
Honey Red Ale

Oregon Original India Pale Ale is heavily hopped with Cascade hops during both the brewing and the dry-hopping, with a hopping rate of nearly a pound and a half per barrel. The crisp spiciness is balanced by the flavors from the malt. A pleasant fruitiness from the specially selected yeast can also be detected in both the aroma and the taste. Oregon Original India Pale Ale has an amber color from the blend of three types of malt.

Oregon Trail Brown Ale

Oregon Trail Brewery
341 S.W. 2nd St.
Corvallis, OR 97333
(541) 758-3527

Other Beers:
Oregon Trail White Ale
Oregon Trail Stout
Oregon Trail Ale
Oregon Trail Pacific Gem Porter

The brown ale tradition evolved from the working-class areas of northern England, where great thirsts developed in the steel mills. Oregon Trail Brown Ale, a flavorful beer, is a blend of crystal, brown, and chocolate malts. The dry, roasty flavor is spiced with Nugget and Willamette hops. It is unpasteurized, with no additives or adjuncts. Good at either end of the trail!

Outrageous Bock

Oldenberg Brewing Company
400 Buttermilk Pike
Fort Mitchell, KY
   41017
(606) 341-7223

Other Beers:
Premium Verum
Holy Grail Nut
   Brown Ale

Outrageous Bock is a traditional rich, dark beer served in the spring or consumed as a late winter warmer. The hearty flavor comes from the large quantities of grain used in this delicious brew. The Oldenberg Brewery, five miles south of Cincinnati, in Fort Mitchell, Kentucky, is home of the American Museum of Brewing History and Arts.

Pacific Golden Ale

Kona Brewing Company
75-5629 Kuakini Hwy.
Kailua-Kona, HI 96740
(808) 334-1133

Other Beers:
Fire Rock Pale Ale

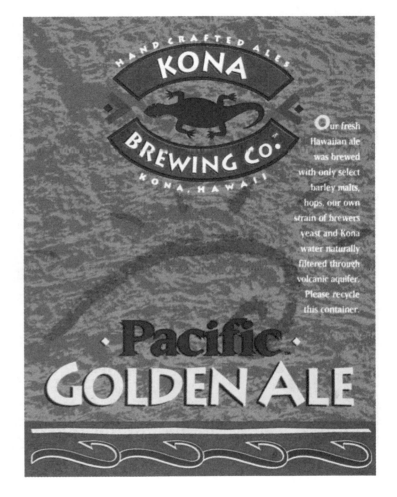

Pacific Golden Ale's refreshing taste comes from a blend of pale and honey malts, finished with a hint of Bullion and Willamette hops. Kona Brewing Company produces fresh Hawaiian ale brewed with their own strain of brewer's yeast and Kona water naturally filtered through a volcanic aquifer.

Page Amber Beer

James Page Brewing Company
1300 Quincy St. N.E.
Minneapolis, MN
  55413
(612) 378-0771

Other Beers:
Wild Rice Lager

James Page Amber Beer is modeled after a traditional Vienna-style lager. It is a full-bodied, aromatic lager characterized by a smooth, malty flavor. It has a warm, copper color and is lightly hopped, which provides a suitable balance to the malt without being overly bitter.

Pecan St. True Bock

**Old City Brewing
Company**
603 W. 13th St.
Suite 1A-345
Austin, TX 78701
(512) 472-BEER

Other Beers:
Pecan St. Lager

NET CONTENTS 1 PINT, 6 FL. OZ.

Pecan St. True Bock is no "mock bock." Pecan St. True Bock continues Old City Brewing Company's tradition of producing classically styled beers. Its rich, malty character is forged by combining chocolate and caramel malts with traditional two-row barley. Bavarian hops round out this perfectly crafted bock. The brewery doesn't treat the term "bock" lightly; 6.5 percent alcohol by volume puts Pecan St. True Bock in the perfect range for a "true" bock beer.

Penn Dark

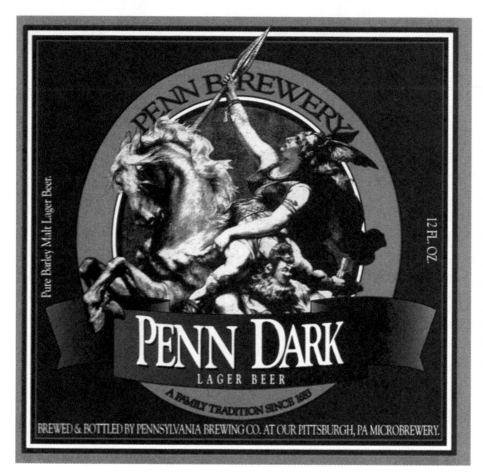

Pennsylvania Brewing Company
800 Vinial St.
Pittsburgh, PA 15212
(412) 237-9400

Other Beers:
Penn Pilsner
Helles Gold
Kaiser Pils
Maerzen
Altbier
Weizen
Weizen Bock
Maibock
All Star Lager
Pastorator
Penn Oktoberfest
St. Nikolaus Bock
  Bier

The Valkyries, so Norse legend goes, conducted slain warriors to Valhalla to spend eternity feasting and drinking, something much like Penn Dark Lager Beer. After all, Penn Brewery makes it just like beers have been brewed in Germany for centuries, using two-row barley malt, Hallertau hops, pure water, yeast, and no preservatives. But it tastes better than the imports, fresher because it's made in Pittsburgh. If you were going to spend eternity drinking beer, this would be the one. Pennsylvania Brewing Company, Pittsburgh's microbrewery.

**Pennsylvania
Brewing Company**
800 Vinial St.
Pittsburgh, PA 15212
(412) 237-9400

Other Beers:
Penn Pilsner
Helles Gold
Kaiser Pils
Maerzen
Altbier
Weizen
Weizen Bock
Maibock
All Star Lager
Pastorator
Penn Dark
St. Nikolaus
    Bock Bier

When Prince Ludwig of Bavaria married Princess Therese on October 12, 1810, the king threw a big party. It was really something. Trumpeters trumpeted. Flag-throwers threw flags. But the best part was the beer. Every year since, all of Munich celebrates all over again, with a festival called Oktoberfest, and a beer just like this one. In Pittsburgh, Penn Brewery hosts the city's most popular Oktoberfest and serves this special beer, made with a rich blend of barley malts and Bavarian Hallertau hops and the original Munich recipe. Enjoy it, and if you feel like offering a toast, repeat after Prince Ludwig: *"Ein Prosit!"*

Perry's Majestic Lager

The Riverosa Company
101 W. 75th St.
Suite 5B
New York, NY
  10023
(212) 721-4566

Perry's Majestic Lager, a richly crafted Vienna lager, is America's first beer to be brewed with organically grown barley and hops. These ingredients are grown without the use of any chemical sprays or fertilizers. The Riverosa Company supports sustainable farming practices and environmental responsibility. That's why they masterfully brew their beer by true traditional methods, using only the finest ingredients available—organically grown barley and hops.

Pete's Wicked Honey Wheat

Pete's Brewing Company
514 High St.
Palo Alto, CA
  94301
(800) 644-7383

Other Pete's Wicked Beers:
Red
Winter Brew
Ale
Lager
Summer Brew

Pete's Wicked Honey Wheat is a richly colored, delicately malted wheat beer flavored with a touch of clover honey. The oldest sweetener in the world, honey, naturally enhances the depth of the caramel malt for a rich, smooth taste. A blend of Tettnang and Cascade hops adds a subtle afterbitter flavor. Pete's Wicked Honey Wheat is unfiltered for a traditional wheat beer experience and a crisp, honey-flavored finish.

215

Pete's Wicked Lager

Pete's Brewing Company
514 High St.
Palo Alto, CA
 94301
(800) 644-7383

Other Pete's Wicked Beers:
Red
Winter Brew
Ale
Summer Brew
Honey Wheat

Pete's Wicked Lager was a 1994 world champion pilsner. A combination of pale and caramel malts gives the lager its full body and rich color. Saaz hops create its signature flavor. The result is a spicy, aromatic pilsner with an inviting hop bitterness. Hop-heads, rejoice!

Pete's Wicked Summer Brew

Pete's Brewing Company
514 High St.
Palo Alto, CA
  94301
(800) 644-7383

Other Pete's Wicked Beers:
Red
Winter Brew
Ale
Lager
Honey Wheat

An authentic pale ale, Pete's Wicked Summer Brew is brewed with pale and wheat malt to create its golden color and classic all-malt flavor. Tettnanger hops deliver a crisp bite, and light carbonation creates a perfect refreshment for an ale fan's summer thirst. A delicate hint of natural lemon flavor is added for a refreshing summer's day taste.

Piccadilly Porter

**The Oxford
Brewing Company**
611 G. Hammonds
 Ferry Rd.
Linthicum, MD
 21090
(410) 789-0005

Other Beers:
Oxford Raspberry-
 Wheat Ale
Oxford Class
 Amber Ale
Oxford Special
 Old Bitter

To re-create this classic English beer style, Oxford uses only British barleys and traditional British hops. The use of darker malts imparts a mahogany hue and coffeelike, almost chocolate, flavor. The brewers infuse the porter with sweeter malts, creating a creamy mouth feel and quaffability. Piccadilly Porter is 5.25% alcohol by volume.

The Pike Brewing Company
1415 First Ave.
Seattle, WA 98101
(206) 622-6044

Other Beers:

Pike Street XXXXX
   Stout

Pike IPA

Auld Acquaintance
   Holiday Ale

The classic Seattle pale ale, Pike Pale Ale is a full-bodied beer with a deep copper color and a nutty malt flavor balanced with an assertive hoppy character. It has delicate fruity esters of peach and apricot. Pike Pale Ale is exceptionally round and mellow, with a very smooth finish. It has been described as "The Cabernet Sauvignon of the Beer World."

Pineapple Ale

Star Brewing Company
5231 N.E. Martin
  Luther King, Jr., Blvd.
Portland, OR 97211
(503) 282-6003

Other Beers:
Elfin Ale
Hop Gold Ale
India Pale Ale
Nut Brown Ale
Raspberry Wheat Ale
Altbier Ale
Black Cherry Stout

The pineapple has long enjoyed a rich and romantic heritage as a symbol of welcome, friendship, and hospitality. Colonial sea captains, returning from their far-reaching travels, often displayed a pineapple at their doors, giving public notice to their friends and acquaintances, "The ship is in! Come join us! Food and drink for all!" Star Pineapple Ale is made with fresh chunk pineapple—one of the few fruits that complements a really refreshing, light beer.

Pintail Extra Special Bitter

Bridgeport Brewing Company
1313 N.W. Marshall St.
Portland, OR 97209
(503) 241-7179

Other Beers:

Coho Pacific Extra Pale Ale

Blue Heron Pale Ale

XX Stout

Old Knucklehead Barleywine

Bridgeport India Pale Ale

Bridgeport Porter

Made with imported Scottish pale malts and whole flower hops, Pintail is dry and aromatic. This golden-hued ale is assertively hopped yet balanced with a rich and refreshing taste. Bridgeport ales are made with two-row malted barley from Oregon and Washington, supplemented by imported English specialty roasted barley malts. Hops from the Pacific Northwest, reputed to be some of the finest hops in the world, also are used in the brewing process. Bridgeport Brewing Company is Oregon's oldest operating microbrewery, and is in Portland, a leading city in the microbrewing renaissance.

Placerville Pale Ale

The Hangtown Brewery

560A Placerville Dr.
Placerville, CA
  95667
(916) 621-3999

Other Beers:

Placerville Summer
  Ale

Stout Ale

Hangtown
  Boysenberry Ale

Placerville Pale Ale is a light ale that starts with a nice hop aroma that complements a subtle fruitiness and slight butterscotch scent. It is full-bodied for its style, with a clean maltiness, a good hop flavor, and a not too overpowering hop finish. The Hangtown Brewery is named after Placerville's nickname, Hangtown. The city earned this name in the miner's days of the American Gold Rush when several "gentlemen" hung from a famous Oak tree.

Stevens Point Brewery
2617 Water St.
Stevens Point, WI
  54481
(715) 344-9310

Other Point Beers:
Pale Ale
Special
Classic Amber
Winter Spice Ale
Maple Wheat

Contrary to the rumors that persist, each batch of Point Bock Beer is brewed-in, just like every batch of beer. It definitely is not the annual spring cleaning of the bottom of the vats. Point Bock Beer is a rich, creamy lager with roasted malts that give it a caramel color and flavor. This is what makes it a genuine bock beer. The body is full but finely balanced, with generous amounts of four varieties of malt and two varieties of hops. The full character of Point Bock Beer is smooth to the palate but leaves a delicious aftertaste.

Poleeko Gold Pale Ale

Anderson Valley Brewing Company
14081 Hwy. 128
P.O. Box 505
Boonville, CA 95415
(707) 895-BEER

Other Beers:
High Rollers Wheat Beer
Boont Amber Ale
Deep Enders Dark Porter
Belk's Extra Special Bitter Ale
Barney Flats Oatmeal Stout
Winter Solstice Select Ale
India Pale Ale
St. David's Belgian Ale
Raspberry Wheat
Millenium Ale

Named for Philo, which is six miles west of Boont, Poleeko Gold is awarded the same devotion for its taste as the Poleeko region gains from its natural beauty. Anderson Valley Brewing Company's honey gold pale ale is crisp and clear, with an unusual lightness and dryness for such a full-flavored drink. A generous addition of Pacific Northwest hops adds both a floral bouquet and a slightly bitter, lively finish.

Big Time Brewing Company

4133 University
   Way, N.E.
Seattle, WA 98105
(206) 545-4509

Other Beers:

Coal Creek Porter

Bhagwan's Best
   India Pale Ale

Old Wooly
   Barleywine Ale

Atlas Amber Ale

Prime Time Pale Ale is the lightest of Big Time's beers. Its pale straw color and gently balanced hoppiness make it easily accessible to those unfamiliar with microbrewed beers, yet its Continental hop finish provides a sophistication that pleases seasoned drinkers of real ales. In 1990, 1992, and 1993 Prime Time Pale Ale was the gold medal winner in the blonde ale category at the Great American Beer Festival® in Denver.

Professor Brewhead's Brown Ale

McNeill's Brewery
90 Elliot St.
Brattleboro, VT
   05301
(802) 254-2553

Other Beers:
Oatmeal Stout
Duck's Breath Ale
Firehouse Amber Ale
Pullman's Porter
Extra Special
   Bitter Ale
Dead Horse India
   Pale Ale

Professor Brewhead's Old Fashioned Brown Ale is handmade from the highest-quality English whole flower hops and Harington barley malt and is made in the style of brown ales of northern England and Scotland. Fully aged and never filtered, this traditional bottle-conditioned ale may contain a small amount of sediment and must be kept refrigerated. For more information about this product write McNeill's Brewery or drop by their pub, open after 4:00 P.M. daily, where you can sample beer directly from the brewery cellars.

Pumpkin Ale

**Buffalo Bill's
Brewery**
Box 510
Hayward, CA
  94543-0510
(510) 538-9500

Other Beers:
Alimony Ale
Diaper Pale Ale
Tasmanian Devil
Hearty Ale
Billy Bock
Krambic

The brewing of Pumpkin Ale was inspired by George Washington, who was an avid "home brewer." Washington used pumpkins and other vegetables in the brewing process. The first of Buffalo Bill's Pumpkin Ale was produced from a forty-pound pumpkin, seeded, and baked at 350°F for three hours. The pumpkin was then added to the mash run on brew day. Its pulp produced starches that convert to sugars, and these sugars are then fermented to produce alcohol. Prior to serving Pumpkin Ale, allspice should be added to give a unique "pumpkin ale" flavor.

Pyramid Espresso Stout

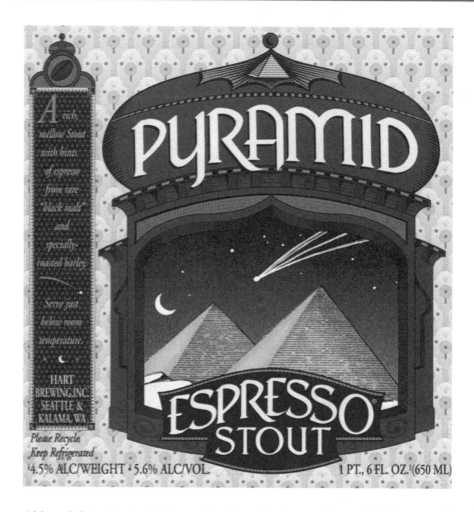

Pyramid Ales
91 S. Royal
  Brougham Way
Seattle, WA 98134
(206) 682-8322

Other Pyramid Beers:
Kälsch
Hefeweizen
Wheaten Ale
Rye Ale
Best Brown
Pale Ale
Apricot Ale
Snow Cap Ale
Anniversary Ale
Porter

Although it isn't actually brewed with coffee beans, Pyramid's Espresso Stout has a tight coffee-colored head and rich layers of coffeeish, chocolatey flavor. Jet-black in color, it is dry, dense, and extremely complex. The *Seattle Times* rates it as simply "outstanding." Pyramid Ales, brewed in Seattle and Kalama, Washington, are among the country's most highly acclaimed specialty beers.

Pyramid Kälsch Beer

Pyramid Ales

91 S. Royal
  Brougham Way
Seattle, WA 98134
(206) 682-8322

Other Pyramid Beers:

Espresso Stout
Hefeweizen
Wheaten Ale
Rye Ale
Best Brown
Pale Ale
Apricot Ale
Snow Cap Ale
Anniversary Ale
Porter

Please Recycle
Keep Refrigerated

Like its German predecessors, Pyramid Kälsch is a pale, light-bodied, almost delicate beer with a hoppy dryness and slightly herbal flavor.

HART
BREWING, INC.®

SEATTLE &
KÄLAMA, WA

KÄLSCH™ BEER
1 PT., 6FL. OZ. (650 ML.)

Inspired by Germany's Kölschbier but named after hometown Kalama! Pyramid's summer seasonal Pyramid Kälsch Beer is soft but firm in body, lightly fruity, with a pleasing, hoppy dryness. A classic German hop variety (Hersbrucker Hallertau) gives this quaffable golden ale its fresh, herbal aroma. Pyramid Ales, brewed in Seattle and Kalama, Washington, are among the country's most highly acclaimed specialty beers.

Raincross Cream Ale

Riverside Brewing Company
1229 Columbia Ave.
Suite C4
Riverside, CA 92507
(909) 682-5465

Other Beers:
Pullman Pale Ale
Victoria Ave.
  Amber Ale
7th Street Stout
Golden Spike Pilsner

Raincross Cream Ale brews to a beautiful gold color and is a pleasant cream ale with a well-hopped aroma and bright hop flavor. The brewers at Riverside Brewing Company think that this ale's good body combined with the long, dry aftertaste make it a natural by itself or with food. This award-winning beer is available year-'round for your enjoyment.

Ram's Head Spring Bock

Coeur d'Alene
Brewing Company
204 N. 2nd St.
Coeur d'Alene, ID
  83814
(208) 664-BREW

Other Beers:
Festival Dark Ale
Centennial Pale Ale
Cherry Porter
Red Oktober
Cream Ale
Light Wheat Beer
Huckleberry Ale

Lagering for more than forty days provides the spring months with a big-tasting, full-bodied Helles Bock from the Coeur d'Alene Brewing Company to you. Incorporating generous amounts of caramel and pale malt with Bullion and Cascade hops produces an enticingly smooth beverage that is sure to lift your spirits after the long winter months.

Raspberry Whacker Wheat Beer

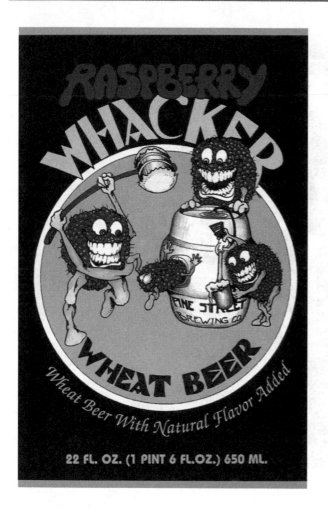

Lonetree Brewing Ltd.
375 E. 55th Ave.
Denver, CO 80216
(303) 297-3832

Other Beers:
Sunset Red Ale
Country Cream Ale
Iron Horse Dark Ale
Snow Dog Ale
Lazy Lizard Wheat
 Beer
Almond Brothers
 Amber Ale
Stone Cold Golden
 Ale
High Point E.S.B.
Horizon Honey Ale
Atlantis Ancient
 Whale Ale
II Angels Chili
 Breeze Ale

Lonetree Brewing packs a whole lot of raspberry flavor into this American-style wheat beer created specially for Pine Street Brewing Company. Raspberry Whacker Wheat Beer is not too strong, but it's not wimpy, either. The brewers at Lonetree have added the purest raspberry extract to the perfect balance of the finest barley, hops, and malted wheat. Whack your taste buds with this super brew—they will love you for it.

James Bay Brewing Company
154 W. Broadway
Port Jefferson, NY
11777
(516) 928-2525

Other Beers:
Drowned Meadow
  Pale Ale
Jefferson Porter
James Bay Winter
  Warmer
Kolsch
Spiced Ale

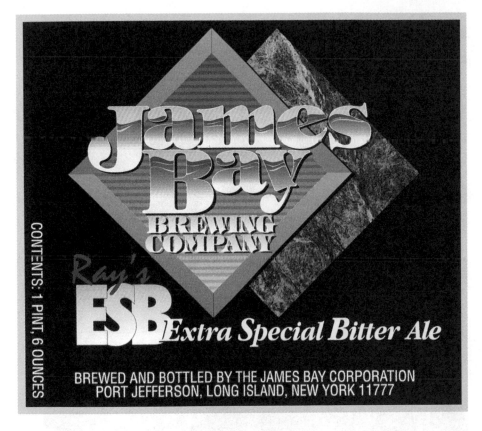

Ray's ESB (extra special bitter) Ale is reminiscent of the style popular in England for many years. James Bay Brewery's version finishes to approximately 3.6 percent alcohol, a little lower than the usual ale, with a slightly sweet aftertaste. Located on scenic Port Jefferson Harbor in New York, James Bay Brewery was the first microbrewery on Long Island.

The Razz

12 FL. OZ (355 ML)

THE RAZZ

Raspberry flavored wheat lager

MUELLER

WHEAT LAGER WITH NATURAL | RASPBERRY FLAVOR

Capital Brewery Company
7734 Terrace Ave.
Middleton, WI
    53562-0185
(608) 836-7100

Other Garten Bräu Beers:
Lager
Special
Dark
Wisconsin Amber
Weizen
Maibock
Oktoberfest
Wild Rice
Winterfest
Doppelbock
Liam Mahoney's
    Brown Ale
Bock

Capital Brewery Company's Raspberry Wheat is an amber-hued beer with the delicious aroma of raspberry. The up-front flavor of raspberry is blended with a rich malt sweetness derived from a blend of wheat and malted barley. The taste sensation is completed with a mild hop character inviting the next sip. The brewery produced its first brew in the spring of 1986 and now has distribution in nine Midwestern states.

**Oaken Barrel
Brewing Company**
50 N. Airport Pkwy.
Suite L
Greenwood, IN 46143
(317) 887-2287

Razz-Wheat is an Americanized version of a Belgian fruit beer. Handcrafted in Greenwood, Indiana, by Oaken Barrel Brewing Company since July 1994, this berried treasure won a silver medal in the fruit beers category at the 1995 Great American Beer Festival®. With a slightly sweet flavor and clean, refreshing finish, this beer is the perfect thirst quencher for the spring and summer.

Red Banshee Ale

1 PINT 6 FL. OZ.

Brewed & Bottled by the H.C. Berger Brewing Co. Ft. Collins,

H. C. Berger Brewing Company
1900 E. Lincoln Ave.
Fort Collins, CO
  80524
(970) 493-9044

Other Beers:
Whistlepin Wheat
Indego Pale Ale
Chocolate Stout
Red Raspberry
  Wheat Ale
Colorado Golden Ale

H. C. Berger Brewing Company is proud to present its Red Banshee Ale, a deep, ruby red ale with a robust, nutty flavor and a nice hop aroma. Red Banshee is a smooth, quaffable ale— "a wailing good brew"! H. C. Berger Brewing Company brews its ales at colder temperatures, using a high degree of blended malts. This provides the palate with the smooth, clean finish that H. C. Berger ales are known for.

RED BELL Blonde Ale

**RED BELL
Brewing Company**
3100 Jefferson St.
Brewerytown-
  Philadelphia, PA
  19121
(888) RED-BELL

Other Beers:
RED BELL Amber
  Lager
India Pale Ale - IPA
Black Cherry Stout
Philadelphia Original
  Lager
Strawberry Mansion
  Wheat
Lemon Hill Wheat

Red Bell Blonde Ale is a pale, golden-colored aromatic beer. This German-style beer is clean-tasting and very drinkable. It is light in body but not on the palate. A small portion of malted wheat is used to give a subtle fruitiness and assist in the head retention. Red Bell Blonde Ale has much more character than a standard American-style lager. Its character is that of Kolsch beers produced in Cologne, Germany. The most attractive feature of this beer is its lightly malty-winey bouquet and gentle flowery hop dryness to the finish.

Red Lady Ale

The Crested Butte Brewery
P.O. Box 1089
Crested Butte, CO
 81224
(303) 349-5027

Other Beers:

White Buffalo
 Peace Ale

Rodeo Stout

Hog Wild Bitter

East India Pale Ale

3 Pin Smoked Porter

Winterlong Ale

Alley Ale

Mc C.S. Scottish Ale

Vinotok Harvest
 Brown Ale

Back in the old mining days of Colorado, the Red Lady was a famous prostitute. Today Red Lady Ale is a robust English-style bitter. Caramel and chocolate malts give this beer a deep copper color. Aggressive hopping with Tettnang and Willamette hops give Red Lady a clean yet slightly bitter finish. Red Lady Ale is The Crested Butte Brewery's flagship brew.

Red Mountain Red Ale

Birmingham Brewing Company
3118 3rd Ave. S.
Birmingham, AL
  35233
(205) 326-6677

Other Beers:
Red Mountain
  Wheat Beer

Beginning with the traditional brewing methods of true English ales, Birmingham Brewing Company steam-brews with a blend of the finest malts and hops. The result is a robust flavor that is at home both in the taverns of Yorkshire and American homes. Birmingham Brewing Company uses no preservatives or additives, so please keep Red Mountain Red Ale chilled for the soonest possible enjoyment.

Red Nectar Ale

**Humboldt Brewing
Company**
856 10th St.
Arcata, CA 95521
(707) 826-1734

Other Beers:
Gold Rush Ale
Oatmeal Stout
Gold Nectar Ale

Red Nectar Ale is Humboldt Brewing Company's flagship ale. It is a robust, red, fruity flower of a beer, in keeping with its name. Its fiery copper color comes from the generous use of imported crystal malt. The "nectar" sweetness is offset by the bitterness and bouquet of Chinook, Mt. Hood, Cascade, and Willamette hops in an aromatic amalgamation.

Red Raspberry Wheat Ale

H. C. Berger Brewing Company
1900 E. Lincoln Ave.
Fort Collins, CO
  80524
(970) 493-9044

Other Beers:
Whistlepin Wheat
Indego Pale Ale
Chocolate Stout
Red Banshee Ale
Colorado Golden Ale

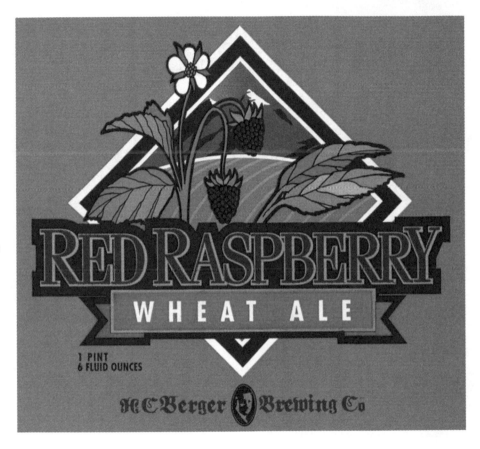

H. C. Berger Brewing Company's Red Raspberry Wheat Ale is a tasty entry into the fruit beer market. This beer is a tangy American wheat ale brewed with a large quantity of fresh red raspberries. Not too sweet, not too tart. H. C. Berger Brewing Company brews its ales at colder temperatures, using a high degree of blended malts. This provides the palate with the smooth, clean finish that H. C. Berger ales are known for.

Red Rock Ale

**Triple Rock
Brewing Company**
1920 Shattuck Ave.
Berkeley, CA 94704
(510) THE-ROCK

Triple Rock Brewing Company, in downtown Berkeley, was one of the nation's first brewpubs, and since it first opened its doors in 1986, its breweriana-filled pub is consistently voted the East Bay's best for its friendly atmosphere and nicely priced pints. Triple Rock Brewing Company now offers ten house-brews including Red Rock Ale, a full-bodied, American-style red ale, and a great accompaniment to a game of shuffleboard!

**North Coast
Brewing Company**
455 N. Main St.
Fort Bragg, CA
 95437
(707) 964-BREW

Other Beers:
Scrimshaw Pilsner
 Style Beer
Old No. 38 Stout
Blue Star Wheat
 Beer

Malt and hops are beautifully married in this full-bodied, copper-red pale ale. Red Seal Ale is generously hopped in the traditional manner for a long, spicy finish and is an excellent accompaniment to grilled meats and rich sauces. This beer has won several awards, including a silver medal at the Great American Beer Festival® in the amber ale category, and gold medals at the 1994 and 1995 World Beer Championships®.

Red Tail Ale

Mendocino Brewing Company
13351 Hwy. 101 S.
P.O. Box 400
Hopland, CA 95449
(707) 744-1015

Other Beers:
Blue Heron Pale Ale
Black Hawk Stout
Frolic Shipwreck Ale
Yuletide Porter
Eye Of The Hawk
    Select Ale
Peregrine Pale Ale
Springtide Ale

The flagship ale of Mendocino Brewing Company of Hopland, California, Red Tail Ale is a full-bodied, slightly dry amber ale brewed in the traditional English style. The recipe uses premium two-row malted barley and whole Cascade and Cluster hops. Red Tail Ale is bottle-conditioned to provide natural flavor. Mendocino Brewing Company was the first brewpub in California and second in the United States since Prohibition.

The Redhook Ale Brewery, Inc.
3400 Phinney Ave. N.
Seattle, WA 98103
(206) 548-8000

Other Beers:
Wheathook Ale
Ballard Bitter IPA
Redhook Rye
Extra Special Bitter
Ale
Blackhook Porter
Winterhook
Christmas Ale
Redhook Double
Black Stout

Redhook ESB is modeled after the premium "extra specials" offered in English pubs. This rich, copper-colored ale has a pleasant finish created by a complex balance between the bitterness of Czechoslovakian Tettnang hops and the sweetness provided by heavier caramel malting. Redhook ESB goes well with cheese dishes, beef, roasted chicken, and all manner of fowl.

Redstone Ale

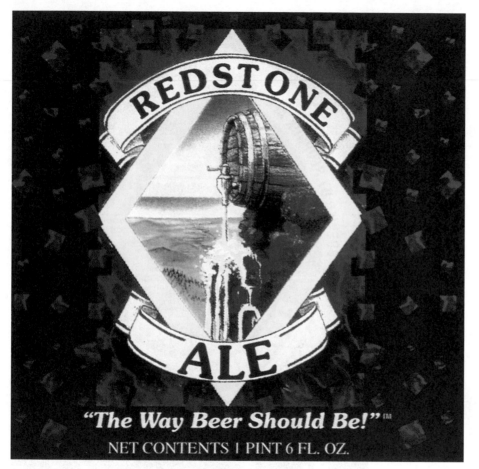

Sunday River Brewing Company
14 York St.
Portland, ME 04101
(207) 773-BEER

Other Beers:
Black Bear Porter

Sunday River Brewing Company's Redstone Ale is undoubtably the local favorite in Bethel and elsewhere in the great state of Maine. Its malty, full-bodied flavor is balanced by generous hoppings of Cascade and Mt. Hood hops. Only the finest domestic raw materials are used to create this authentic American-styled ale.

Rikenjaks E.S.B.

Rikenjaks Brewing Company
P.O. Box 53528
Lafayette, LA 70505
(318) 233-2802

Other Beers:
American Ale
Old Hardhead

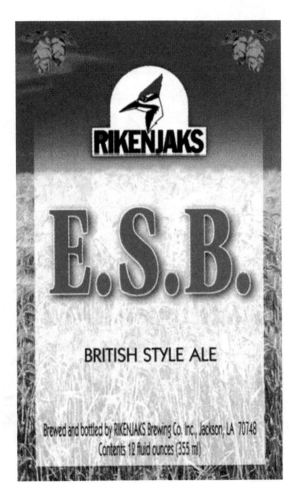

Rikenjaks E.S.B. is a British-Style ale with an amber color and a complex caramel malt balance, which derives from the nine brewer's malts used in its production. The Rikenjaks Brewery's E.S.B. is firmly hopped in the kettle and finished with Goldings, the classic British hop. At Rikenjaks a great deal of attention is paid to the details of brewing fine beer. It is this special commitment that makes each of their products a classic example of its respective beer style.

Riverwest Stein Beer

Lakefront Brewery, Inc.
818A E. Chambers St.
Milwaukee, WI 53212
(414) 372-8800

Other Beers:
Cream City Pale Ale
Klisch Pilsner
East Side Dark
Lakefront Cherry Beer
Lakefront Bock Beer
Lakefront Holiday Spice

The rich amber color and caramel flavor of Riverwest Stein are derived from the generous amount of caramel malt in this recipe, with just a dash of roasted, unmalted barley for a subtle toasted flavor in the background. The sweetness, body, and mouth feel tell you that this is an all-malt beer. The finish has a balanced edge of bitter hoppiness that cuts through the malty character, leaving a clean palate that beckons for more. Lakefront uses a blend of fine domestic and imported hops to achieve this marriage of contrasting flavors.

Saint Arnold Brown Ale

**Saint Arnold
Brewing Company**
2522 Fairway Park Dr.
Houston, TX 77092
(713) 686-9494

Other Beers:
Saint Arnold Kristall
  Weizen
Saint Arnold Amber
  Ale

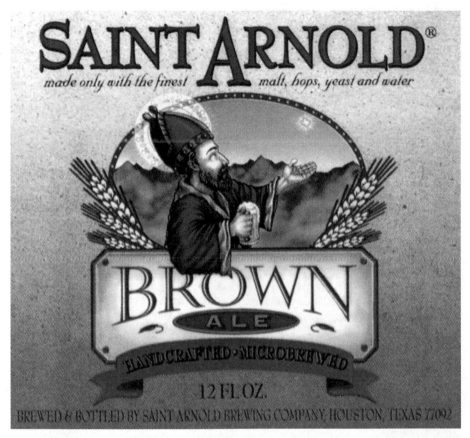

Saint Arnold Brewing Company is Houston's first microbrewery. The brewery is named for the patron saint of brewers, Saint Arnold, a Catholic bishop who warned of the dangers of drinking water and extolled the virtues of beer. For more information about the brewery's products, call (800) 801-6402. Also, check out their home page at http://www.saintarnold.com/saintarnold.

St. James Ale

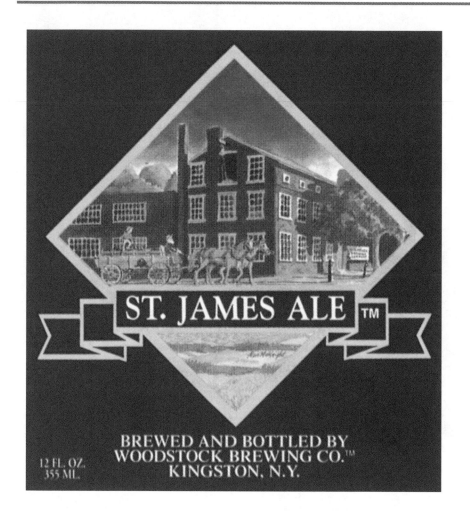

Woodstock Brewing Company
P.O. Box 1000W
20 St. James St.
Kingston, NY 12401
(914) 331-2810

Other Beers:
Hudson Lager
Big Indian Porter
Ichabod Crane
   Holiday Lager

St. James Ale is clean and crisp, with a flowery aroma; a thick, creamy head; and a rich, gold color. St. James Ale is a classical example of a true American beer. Cheers! The brick structure that houses the brewery was built in about 1830 as the Hermance Foundry. Later it became the Ulster Foundry, and it continued to operate as such until the 1950s. Today the interior has been totally refurbished and contains Woodstock Brewing Company's 6,000 square-foot traditional brewing operation.

St. Nikolaus Bock Bier

Pennsylvania Brewing Company
800 Vinial St.
Pittsburgh, PA 15212
(412) 237-9400

Other Beers:
Penn Pilsner
Helles Gold
Kaiser Pils
Maerzen
Altbier
Weizen
Weizen Bock
Maibock
All Star Lager
Pastorator
Penn Oktoberfest
Penn Dark

At the start of the nineteenth century he was a tall, stern patriarch in bishop's robes. Today he's a jolly, globular, sky-riding elf. St. Nick may be a milk-and-cookies kind of guy, but he knows what you want, and it's Penn Brewery's St. Nikolaus Bock Bier. Rich, dark and full-bodied, because it's brewed just like beers are brewed in Germany, with a blend of roasted barley malts and Bavarian Hallertau hops. It's fresher, though, because it's made in Pittsburgh. Sure hope you've been good this year!

St. Stan's Amber Alt

St. Stan's Brewing Company
821 L St.
Modesto, CA 95354
(209) 524-BEER

Other St. Stan's Beers:
Dark Alt
Fest Beer
Whistle Stop Pale Ale
Red Sky Ale
Graffiti Wheat

St. Stan's Amber Alt is made in the *Altbier* style of Düsseldorf, Germany, with low carbonation and a smooth, malty, nonbitter taste. The beer is amber in color with a creamy, smooth flavor. The bittering hops are Cascades and Fuggles and the aromatics are Cascades and Tettnang. This beer is naturally pristine and pleasing to the palate. St. Stan's Brewing Company offers a beer for all tastes.

Sara's Brown Ale

Yegua Creek Brewing Company
2920 N. Henderson Ave.
Dallas, TX 75206
(214) 824-BREW

Other Beers:
Tucker's Golden Wheat
Lucky Lady Lager
Xit Pilsner
Ice Haus Pale Ale
White Rock Red
O'Brien's Texas Stout
Big D ESB

Sara's Brown Ale was a 1994 Great American Beer Festival® gold medal brew in the English brown ale category. It has malty flavor balanced by low hop bitterness, which bring out the slight chocolate finish. Best in Texas, best in the United States, best ever. Yegua Creek Brewing Company is housed in a seventy-year-old icehouse located near downtown Dallas.

Saranac Adirondack Amber

F. X. Matt Brewing Company
811 Edward St.
Utica, NY
  13502-4092
(315) 732-3181

Other Saranac Beers:
Black & Tan
Pale Ale
Golden Pilsener
Season's Best
Black Forest
Chocolate Amber
Mountain Berry Ale

Saranac Adirondack Amber is naturally krausened and lagered. This classic German-style amber lager carefully balances the sweetness of all-two-row malt with the delicate bitterness of carefully chosen hops and pure Adirondack water. The result is a perfectly balanced, full-flavored beer that wins awards and accolades at tastings around the United States.

Saranac Golden Pilsener

F. X. Matt Brewing Company
811 Edward St.
Utica, NY
   13502-4092
(315) 732-3181

Other Saranac Beers:
Black & Tan
Pale Ale
Adirondack Amber
Season's Best
Black Forest
Chocolate Amber
Mountain Berry Ale

Saranac Golden Pilsener is a smooth, crisp beer made with two-row barley and wheat malts and Cascade and Tettnanger hops. This beer is "dry-hopped" during aging, which creates a distinctive hop nose and flavor. Look for a pleasant, mild taste with a slightly aromatic trademark finish; very refreshing. The F. X. Matt Brewing Company was founded in 1888.

Schild Brau Amber

Millstream Brewing Company
P.O. Box 284
Amana, IA 52203
(319) 622-3672

Other Beers:
Millstream Wheat
  Beer
Millstream Lager
  Beer

As the name suggests, Schild Brau is a beer radiating the richness of premium European brew. Reminiscent of the special Oktoberfest beers of Munich, Schild Brau Amber achieves its own distinctive flavor and quality. Schild Brau Amber should be savored so that each nuance of its character can be experienced. The tiny, fabled Millstream Brewery is located on an actual millstream in the main village of Amana and is one of the oldest operating microbreweries in the United States, opening in 1985.

Screaming Lobster Lager

Southern California Brewing Company

833 W. Torrance Blvd.
Suite 4
Torrance, CA 90502
(310) 329-8881

Other Beers:

Olde Red Eye Red Ale

California Light
  Blonde Lager

Honey Wheat Ale

Bear Country
  Heife Weizen

Buck Horn Bock

Winter Wonder

Southern California Brewing Company uses five different two-row barley malts in Screaming Lobster Lager. These malts are blended, based on their assays, in order to obtain a true Continental lager profile. The spice of the beer is provided by imported Hersbrucker hops that are grown in the famous Hallertau region in northern Bavaria. Screaming Lobster Lager has a full body with a malty palate that should appeal to the beer drinker who has experienced good beer fresh from the brewery in Germany.

Settlers Ale

Crooked River Brewing Company
1101 Center St.
Cleveland, OH
  44113
(206) 771-2337

Other Beers:
Black Forest Lager
Lighthouse Gold
Cool Mule Porter
Irish Red
Erie Nights Pumpkin
  Brew
Doppelbock
Yuletide Ale
Bicentennial Hefe-
  Weizen

Early Clevelanders enjoyed vigorous lives, with beers to match their robust existence. Today the character of these original Cleveland brews lives again in Settlers Ale, proudly brewed by Crooked River Brewing Company. Crooked River Settlers Ale is a traditionally crafted English ale with a hoppy zest that makes every sip a pleasure. Amber in color, this hearty, full-bodied ale is rich and robust with a smooth, clean finish.

Shiner Bock Beer

Spoetzl Brewery
14800 San Pedro, #310
San Antonio, TX 78232
(210) 490-9128

Other Beers:
Kosmos Reserve Lager

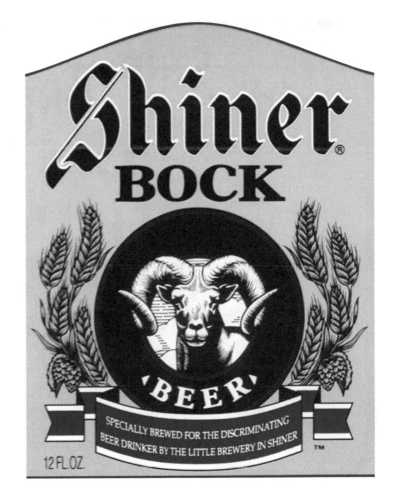

Shiner Bock Beer is a rich, smooth, dark lager that has become a Texas legend. It was originally brewed only seasonally, but its popularity grew tremendously, and in 1975 it was brewed year-'round to meet the demands of their customers. Shiner Bock Beer is specially brewed for the discriminating beer drinker by the little brewery in Shiner, TX.

Shipyard Export Ale

Shipyard Brewing Company
86 Newbury St.
Portland, ME 04101
(800) 273-9253

Other Beers:
Goat Island Light Ale
Blue Fin Stout
Old Thumper
Shipyard Brown Ale
Chamberlain Pale Ale
Longfellow Winter Ale
Mystic Seaport
   Pale Ale
Prelude Ale
Longfellow India
   Pale Ale
Sirius Summer
   Wheat Ale

Shipyard Brewing Company is New England's premier microbrewery and is on Portland, Maine's, historic waterfront. They use handcrafted and time-honored traditional brewing methods to create their award-winning microbrews. Shipyard Export Ale is golden copper in hue and malty, with a hint of sweetness up front and a dry, hoppy finish. Shipyard Brewing Company uses only the finest all-natural ingredients in their ales because they are committed to brewing the freshest, most flavorful, and full-bodied ales available. Enjoy with their best wishes!

Shoals Pale Ale

Smuttynose Brewing Company
225 Heritage Ave.
Portsmouth, NH 03801
(603) 436-4026

Other Beers:
Old Brown Dog Ale

The Samuel Haley house on Smuttynose Island

Smuttynose Brewing Company is named for Smuttynose Island, part of a small, rugged archipelago that lies off the coast of New Hampshire. Smuttynose Brewing Company brews its ales by hand, using time-honored methods and the finest ingredients, right in the seacoast city of Portsmouth, New Hampshire. Shoals Pale Ale is a rich, copper-colored ale with an assertive hop flavor and fragrance. Brewed with English malt and American hops, it is unfiltered, unpasteurized, and naturally carbonated for a fresh, delicious flavor. Don't settle for just any beer. Next time tell the bartender, "Make mine a Smutty!"

Sierra Nevada Pale Ale

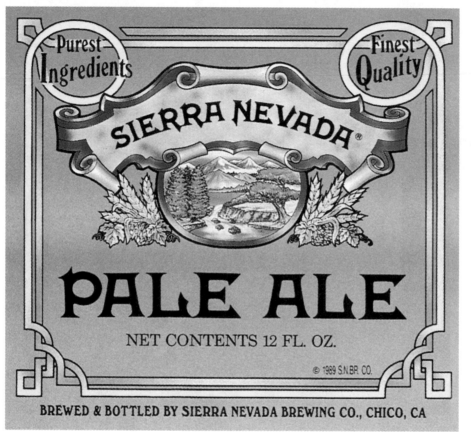

Sierra Nevada Brewing Company
1075 E. 20th St.
Chico, CA 95928
(916) 893-3520

Other Sierra Nevada Beers:
Pale Bock
Summerfest
Celebration Ale
Porter
Stout
Bigfoot Ale

Sierra Nevada Pale Ale is a delightful example of the classic pale ale style. It has a deep amber color and an exceptionally full-bodied, complex character. The fragrant bouquet and spicy flavor are the results of the generous use of the best Cascade hops. The next time you are in northern California, stop by and see the beer being made at the Sierra Nevada Brewing Company.

**Sierra Nevada
Brewing Company**
1075 E. 20th St.
Chico, CA 95928
(916) 893-3520

**Other Sierra
Nevada Beers:**
Pale Bock
Summerfest
Celebration Ale
Porter
Pale Ale
Bigfoot Ale

Sierra Nevada Stout is a creamy and full-bodied example of this traditional-style ale. Very dark and very rich, this stout displays a pronounced roasted flavor. Sierra Nevada Brewing Company was conceived with the one simple goal of brewing the finest ales and lagers possible. Their success can be measured by the many awards they have won.

Simpatico Amber

Dubuque Brewing Company
500 E. 4th St.
Dubuque, IA
   52001-2398
(319) 583-2042

Other Beers:
Simpatico Lager

The spanish word *simpático* means "in harmony," which is a good description of Simpatico Amber's color, malt, and hoppiness. It is a classic Vienna-styled amber lager brewed by Dubuque Brewing Company and combining pale and caramel malts with Tettnanger hops. True to the Viennese style, it is distinguished by a deep copper color; rich, smooth malt flavor; and soft finish. A gold medal winner at the 1995 World Beer Championships®.

Snow Dog Ale

Lonetree Brewing Ltd.

375 E. 55th Ave.
Denver, CO 80216
(303) 297-3832

Other Beers:

Sunset Red Ale

Country Cream Ale

Iron Horse Dark Ale

Raspberry Whacker
Wheat Beer

Lazy Lizard Wheat
Beer

Almond Brothers
Amber Ale

Stone Cold Golden Ale

High Point E.S.B.

Horizon Honey Ale

Atlantis Ancient
Whale Ale

II Angels Chili Breeze
Ale

The legend of the snow dog originated high in the farthest reaches of the Colorado Rockies. The trappers and miners used to tell of a large white dog who would appear and lead them to safety through blinding snowstorms. Sightings of the snow dog persist, and her memory is kept alive by Snow Dog Ale, a classic handcrafted ale brewed right where her spirit still roams. This beer is brewed exclusively for Snow Dog Brewery Corporation in Avon, Colorado.

Snow Goose Winter Ale

Wild Goose Brewery
20 Washington St.
Cambridge, MD 21613
(410) 221-1121

Other Wild Goose Beers:
Porter
Spring Wheat Ale
India Pale Ale
Amber Ale
Golden Ale

From Thanksgiving through the beginning of the New Year comes Snow Goose Winter Ale, Wild Goose Brewery's most popular seasonal beer. Snow Goose Winter Ale is a traditional English old ale of nearly 7 percent alcohol by volume. A grist of British pale, crystal, and chocolate malts and roasted unmalted barley give Snow Goose a deep brown color with a dry, toasty body and a blend of Cascade, Willamette, Fuggles, and Goldings hops to round out a vibrant finish.

Marthasville Brewing Company
3960 Shirley Drive S.W.
Atlanta, GA 30336
(404) 713-0333

Other Beers:
Sweet Georgia Brown Ale
Classic Ale

Southern Ale is a true ale with a flavor as smooth as the old South. Brewed to please those new to real ales and still be praised by beer connoisseurs. The first shipment of draft beer in June 1994 made Marthasville Brewing Company the first microbrewery in production in the state of Georgia. Since then the company has grown steadily. Just say "Make mine a Martha's!"

Starved Rock Amber Ale

Star Union Brewing Company
P.O. Box 282
Hennepin, IL 61327
(815) 925-7400

Other Beers:
Lincoln Red Ale

Thousands of years ago, the melting glaciers reshaped the face of the Illinois Valley by creating an extraordinary landscape of deep canyons and towering bluffs. Taking its name from ancient Indian lore, Starved Rock is still a place of awe-inspiring beauty. Star Union Brewing Company has created another exceptional beer and named it after this special place: Starved Rock Amber Ale, a rich, hearty ale with a refreshingly smooth taste. Handcrafted in small batches, it's brewed from choice blends of barley and crystal malts, the finest hops, and the purest cultured yeast.

Mad River Brewing Company
P.O. Box 767
Blue Lake, CA 95525
(707) 668-4151

Other Beers:
Steelhead Extra Pale Ale

Jamaica Red

John Barleycorn Barleywine Style Ale

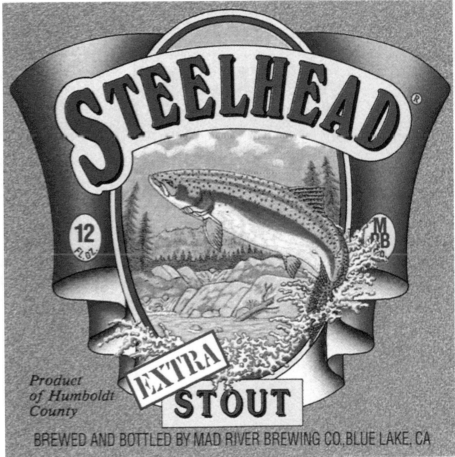

Mad River Brewing Company's Steelhead Extra Stout is a rich, creamy, full-bodied stout with a pleasing chocolate and toasted malt character. Look for Steelhead ales in bottles or on draught at select locations. Kegs and case sales are available at the brewery's retail sales office in Blue Lake, California.

Stegmaier Porter

The Lion Brewery, Inc.
700 N. Pennsylvania Ave.
P.O. Box GS
Wilkes-Barre, PA 18703
(800) 233-8327

Other Beers:
1857 Premium Lager
Brewery Hill Black
  & Tan
Brewery Hill Honey
  Amber Ale
Brewery Hill Raspberry
  Red Ale
Liebotschaner Cream Ale
Brewery Hill Pale Ale
Brewery Hill Cherry
  Wheat

Stegmaier Porter creates a new standard for American dark beer. The brewers at The Lion use two varieties of roasted malt together with two kinds of pale malt to create a deep, dark color and flavor. The finest aroma hops offer a unique balance. Taste the magic of Stegmaier Porter, a product of The Lion Brewery, Wilkes-Barre, Pennsylvania.

**Marin Brewing
Company**
1809 Larkspur
   Landing Circle
Larkspur, CA 94939
(415) 461-4677

Other Beers:
Mt. Tam Pale Ale
Marin Weiss
Marin Hefe Wiess
Blueberry Ale
Raspberry Ale
Albion Amber Ale
San Quentin's
   Breakout Stout
Pt. Reyes Porter
Old Dipsea
   Barleywine
Marin Doppel
   Weizen

Marin Brewing Company's Stinson Beach Peach is a light and refreshing ale that has a wonderful peach nose and is full of peach flavor. Marin uses only 100 percent American ingredients: malt from Washington and Wisconsin, hops from the Yakima Valley in Washington, Marin County's own water, and a carefully selected yeast strain. Taste the American brewing renaissance.

Stoney's Beer

Jones Brewing Company
254 2nd St.
P.O. Box 746
Smithton, PA 15479
(412) 872-BEER

Other Beers:
Stoney's Light

Stoney's Beer, a Jones Brewing Company product, is brewed in the traditional Old World manner from the finest brewer's malt grits and hops to produce a smooth-tasting lager without using syrups, additives, or preservatives. This American Lager is brewed and aged the natural, costlier way for your enjoyment.

Stoudt's Fat Dog Stout

Stoudt Brewing Company
P.O. Box 880
Adamstown, PA
  19501
(717) 484-4387

Other Stoudt's Beers:
Honey Double Bock
PILS
Amber
Abbey Triple
Gold
Honey Double
  Mai Bock
Abbey Double
Fest (Märzen Style)
Scarlet Lady E.S.B.
German Hefeweizen

STOUDT'S™

Since 1987

FAT DOG STOUT

UNFILTERED STOUT BREWED WITH HONEY

MICRO-BREWED
All Natural Ingredients • No Additives or Preservatives

MICROBREWED AND BOTTLED
BY STOUDT BREWING COMPANY
ADAMSTOWN, PA 19501-0800

1 PINT, 9.87 FL. OZ. (765 ML)

Enjoy the world-class flavor of Stoudt's Reserve ales and lagers. Stoudt's Fat Dog Stout is the darkest of Stoudt Brewing Company's ales. It has the traditional imperial style of a stout and is named after a 150-pound Labrador retriever, Ferdinand. This beer won a silver medal in the 1996 World Beer Championships®. You are welcome to visit the brewery, off Pennsylvania Turnpike, exit 21, between Lancaster and Reading.

Stoudt's Honey Double Bock

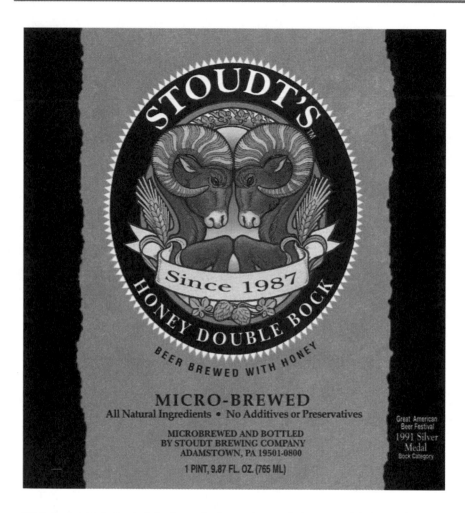

Stoudt Brewing Company
P.O. Box 880
Adamstown, PA 19501
(717) 484-4387

Other Stoudt's Beers:
Fat Dog Stout
PILS
Amber
Abbey Triple
Gold
Honey Double
  Mai Bock
Abbey Double
Fest (Märzen Style)
Scarlet Lady E.S.B.
German Hefeweizen

This beautiful *dunkel* dark-style lager is reminiscent of the monk-style *doppel* bock beers. Stoudt's Honey Double Bock is very malty, full-bodied, and brewed with a touch of honey bottom-fermented lager that just might incline you to search for a goblet to drink it from. This beer won a silver medal in the 1996 World Beer Championships®. *Prosit!* When it began operations in 1987 Stoudt Brewing Company was the first micro operation in Pennsylvania since Prohibition.

Stoudt's PILS

Stoudt Brewing Company
P.O. Box 880
Adamstown, PA 19501
(717) 484-4387

Other Stoudt's Beers:
Fat Dog Stout
Honey Double Bock
Amber
Abbey Triple
Gold
Honey Double
  Mai Bock
Abbey Double
Fest (Märzen Style)
Scarlet Lady E.S.B.
German Hefeweizen

The driest and most delicate of Stoudt Brewing Company's lagers. PILS is characteristic of German, and Czechoslovakian pilsner styles. Assertively hopped with Saaz. Awarded a gold medal in 1993 and 1994 and a bronze medal in 1995 in the European pilsner category at the Great American Beer Festival®. Stoudt Brewing Company still savors its growing reputation for producing some of America's most luscious beers.

Sun Valley Octoberfest

Sun Valley Brewing Company
202 N. Main St.
P.O. Box 389
Hailey, ID 83333
(208) 788-5777

Other Sun Valley Beers:
Gold Lager
Blonde Lager
Our Holiday Ale
Honey Weizen
White Cloud Ale

Fall comes in with a change of colors and a chill in the air. Sun Valley Brewing Company celebrates this change of season with their celebrated Octoberfest, a traditional Vienna-style beer created to celebrate the harvest and the arrival of fall. Also referred to as a Marzen or Vienna export beer, it is characterized by a respectable strength, a smooth and slightly malty palate, and an exquisite reddish color. Enjoy the change of seasons and the colors of fall with a robust and refreshing Octoberfest.

Dry Town Brewery
3 Round House Rd.
Oneonta, NY 13820
(800) DRY-TOWN

Other Beers:
Upstate Amber

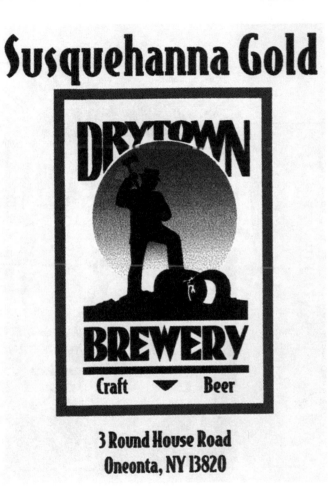

Dry Town Brewery brewed its first batch of Susquehanna Gold on July 27, 1995. This is a traditional British ale with a hearty flavor. The brewery has begun production of its second beer, Upstate Amber, a robust, malty beer. This beer made its debut in October 1995.

Sweet Georgia Brown Ale

Marthasville Brewing Company
3960 Shirley Drive S.W.
Atlanta, GA 30336
(404) 713-0333

Other Beers:
Southern Ale
Classic Ale

Martha's Sweet Georgia Brown Ale is medium-dark and brewed with orange blossom honey to give it a light, sweet taste. The recipe was based on requests from Georgia residents who wanted something special! The first shipment of draft beer in June 1994 made Marthasville Brewing Company the first microbrewery in production in the state of Georgia. Since then the company has grown steadily. Just say "Make mine a Martha's!"

Taildragger Honey Wheat

**Lang Creek
Brewery**
655 Lang Creek Rd.
Marion, MT 59925
(406) 858-2200

Other Beers:
Windsock Pale Ale

Taildragger Honey Wheat is a delightfully rich, tasty, copper-colored ale, medium-hopped with Mt. Hood, Cascade, and Perle hops to provide a delicate balance among several types of malted barley, wheat, and pure Montana honey. A careful inspection of the aroma will reveal a hint of citrus and a slight fragrance of honey. The aftertaste is clean and leaves behind the flavor your nose told you to expect. Your tastebuds will think they've died and gone to heaven.

Tenpenny American Bitter

Boulevard Brewing Company
2501 Southwest Blvd.
Kansas City, MO
  64108
(816) 474-7095

Other Boulevard Beers:
Pale Ale

Wheat Beer

Unfiltered Wheat
  Beer

Bob's '47

Irish Ale

Bully! Porter

Boulevard Tenpenny American Bitter is a mild, refreshing ale, light amber in color, with a pronounced hop flavor and aroma. Tenpenny is Boulevard Brewing Company's rendition of the classic bitter style, the most prevalent type of beer sold on draught in British pubs. Boulevard Brewing Company prides itself as Missouri's second-largest brewery.

Thomas Kemper Bohemian Dunkel

Thomas Kemper Lagers

91 S. Royal
  Brougham Way
Seattle, WA 98134
(206) 682-8322

Other Thomas Kemper Beers:

Hefeweizen

WeizenBerry

Helles Blueberry
  Lager

Pale Lager

Amber Lager

Honey Weizen

WinterBräu

Oktoberfest

White Beer

Mai-Bock

Brewed in the tradition of Bohemia's *dunkel* (dark) lagers, Thomas Kemper Bohemian Dunkel is medium-bodied with a malty-sweet flavor (caramel, chocolate) carefully balanced by spicy Styrian finishing hops. Its attractive reddish-brown color is carefully generated using a blend of five special barley malts. Brewed in Seattle and Poulsbo, Washington, Thomas Kemper Lagers are among the country's most authentic European-style specialty beers.

Tremont India Pale Ale (IPA)

Atlantic Coast Brewing Ltd.
50 Terminal St.
Boston, MA 02129
(617) 242-6464

Other Beers:
Tremont Ale

Tremont India Pale Ale (IPA) is brewed with English malt, English Fuggles, and Styrian Goldings hops. It has a deep golden color and is dominated by a distinctive hop aroma and flavor. Tremont Brewery, in the Charlestown neighborhood of Boston, brews English-style ales and distributes only in the Boston area.

Truckee Brewing Company
11401 Donner Pass Rd.
Truckee, CA 96160
(916) 587-5406

Other Beers:
Boca Bock Lager
Truckee Amber Lager

"Smooth," "pure-tasting," and "round" are some of the adjectives used by the brewery's customers to describe this delectable beer, brewed in one of our nation's coldest spots. A perfectly matched cold weather for a handcrafted cold lager. All malt, all taste, it has the hopping you expect in a true German lager. Truckee Brewing Company has been in operation since 1984 and offers tours of the brewery to the public.

Turbodog

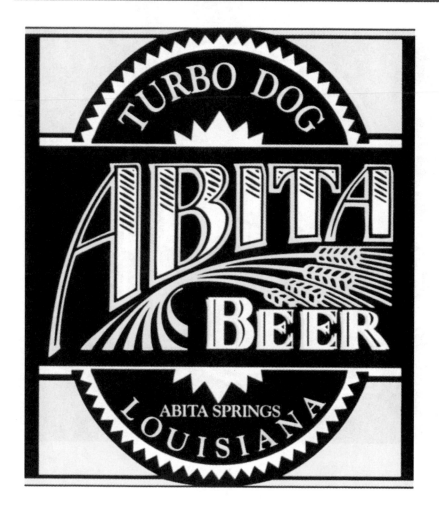

The Abita Brewing Company
P.O. Box 762
Abita Springs, LA
 70420
(800) 737-2311

Other Beers:
Abita Amber
Abita Golden
Abita Red Ale
Abita Wheat
Fall Fest
Purple Haze
XXX-Mas Ale
Abita Bock

Turbodog, first unleashed in 1990, is a dark brown ale brewed with Willamette hops and a combination of pale, caramel, and chocolate malts. The "Dog" began as a specialty ale but gained a huge loyal following and soon became one of The Abita Brewing Company's three standard brews. It is sweeter and has a higher alcohol content than Amber and Golden.

**Tuscan Brewing
Company Inc.**
25009 Kauffman Ave.
Red Bluff, CA 96080
(916) 529-9318

Tuscan Pale Ale is handcrafted from a blend of the finest malted barleys, whole hops, select grains, yeast, and crystal-clear well water from the base of the Tuscan Buttes, not far from the site of the once-famous Tuscan Springs Resort. The resort, which consisted of a three-story hotel, saloon, bathhouse, and rental cottages, was destroyed by fire for the second time on August 22, 1916, and was never rebuilt.

Tut Brown Ale

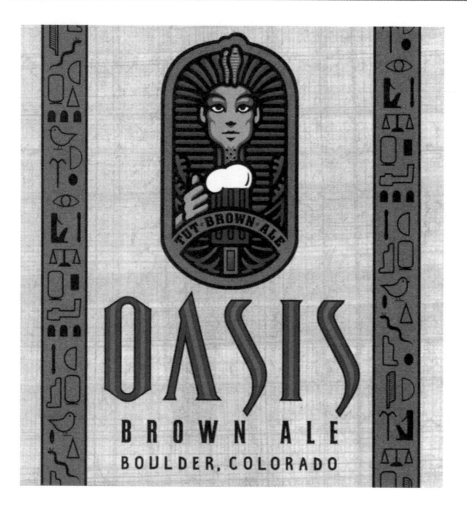

Oasis Brewery
3201 Walnut St. #A
Boulder, CO 80301
(303) 440-8030

Other Beers:
Oasis Pale Ale
Scarab Red
Capstone E.S.B.
Zoser Oatmeal Stout

Oasis Brewery opened the Oasis Annex on Walnut Street in December 1994. The new facility, with a tasting room, serves as the production and bottling plant to distribute to out-of-state wholesalers and service the Colorado area. Oasis's Tut Brown Ale is a sweet, nut-brown ale, rich in caramel malt with a hint of floral hoppiness, absolutely the one to try if you're not quite sure about "dark" beer. This beer was a 1994 Great American Beer Festival® silver medalist in the American brown ale category.

Vail Pale Ale

Hubcap Brewery
P.O. Box 3333
Vail, CO 81658
(970) 476-5757

Other Beers:
Killer Bee Honey Ale

Disciplined by the ancient sixteenth-century German purity law Reinheitsgebot, Hubcap Brewery bottles fewer than 600 barrels of these limited-production handcrafted ales annually. Artisan brewers carefully perfect each recipe, using only the freshest and finest barley, hops, yeast, and pure Vail water. Vail Pale Ale is a very hoppy beer. Massive quantities of Centennial and Cascade hops are added to the kettle, followed by three weeks of additional dry hopping to produce this award-winning beer. Enjoy!

Wasatch Premium Ale

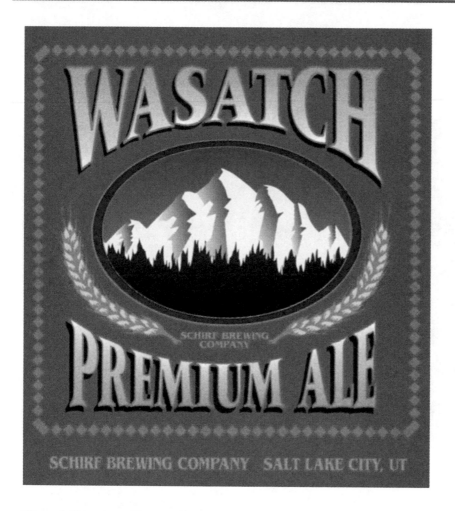

Schirf Brewing Company
P.O. Box 459
250 Main St.
Park City, UT 84060
(801) 645-9500

Other Wasatch Beers:
Raspberry Wheat
Slickrock Lager

Wasatch Premium Ale was the first and remains the number one microbrewed beer in Utah. This amber-colored, full-bodied ale is brewed with a collection of dark kilned malts. Its well-balanced finish is the result of Chinook and Cascade hops.

Wasatch Slickrock Lager

Schirf Brewing Company
P.O. Box 459
250 Main St.
Park City, UT 84060
(801) 645-9500

Other Wasatch Beers:
Raspberry Wheat
Premium Ale

Utah's premium light beer just got better. Brewed with Bavarian yeast and Saaz hops and matured for up to forty-five days, this crisp lager quenches your thirst with genuine Old World character and smoothness. Schirf Brewing Company is also proud of its Wasatch Raspberry Wheat and Wasatch Premium Ale.

White Buffalo Peace Ale

The Crested Butte Brewery
P.O. Box 1089
Crested Butte, CO
  81224
(303) 349-5027

Other Beers:
Red Lady Ale
Rodeo Stout
Hog Wild Bitter
East India Pale Ale
3 Pin Smoked Porter
Winterlong Ale
Alley Ale
Mc C.S. Scottish Ale
Vinotok Harvest
  Brown Ale

The Crested Butte Brewery's White Buffalo Peace Ale is an American-style pale ale, hoppy and fruity with a crisp finish. The brewers at Crested Butte use Munich malt and Cascade hops to give White Buffalo its distinct yet light character. The folks at The Crested Butte Brewery feed their spent grains to the white buffalo there in the valley.

Sun Valley Brewing Company
202 N. Main St.
P.O. Box 389
Hailey, ID 83333
(208) 788-5777

Other Sun Valley Beers:
Gold Lager
Blonde Lager
Our Holiday Ale
Honey Weizen
Octoberfest

White Cloud Ale is a medium-bodied, all-season ale with a deep amber color. It is made from only the finest two-row roasted barley, local Cascade and imported German Hallertau hops, water, and yeast. Perfect for an afternoon's respite, a refreshing complement to the evening's meal, or to cut the thirst after a spin on the dance floor. Sit back, relax, and slip back in time to the cool, refreshing, uninhibited taste of a White Cloud Ale.

White Knight Light Ale

Quench your QUEST. This crisp, refreshing golden ale is traditionally handcrafted in our small brewery. Cheers!

AVERAGE ANALYSIS PER 12 FL. OZ. : CALORIES 129, CARBOHYDRATES 11.5 GRAMS, PROTEIN 1.0 GRAMS, FAT 0.0 GRAMS

White Knight™ Light Ale

BREWED AND BOTTLED BY MIDDLE AGES BREWING CO. LTD. SYRACUSE, NEW YORK USA

12 FL. OZ.

Middle Ages Brewing Company, Ltd.
120 Wilkinson St.
Syracuse, NY 13204
(315) 476-4250

Other Beers:
Grail Ale
Wizard's Winter Ale
Beast Bitter

White Knight Light Ale, Middle Ages Brewing Company's golden ale, is handcrafted in the tradition of a British-style ale (a session beer). This fresh-tasting, thirst-quenching ale is characterized by a delicate balance between the rich malt flavor and the crisp hop finish. White Knight Light Ale is a perfect choice for social occasions and complements salads, vegetables, seafood, and chicken.

Whitetail Maple Wheat Ale

Whitetail Brewing Company
1600 Pennsylvania Ave.
York, PA 17404
(717) 843-6520

Whitetail Maple Wheat Ale is brewed with malted wheat and several specialty malts, with a generous addition of pure dark amber maple syrup from western Pennsylvania. It is balanced with the freshest American-grown hops that are hand-delivered from the Pacific Northwest. This combination creates a fine amber-colored ale with superior head retention and a complex taste with both a fresh hop and maple aroma. This smooth flavor finishes clean with a hint of maple sweetness. Expect to want another!

Wild Boar Classic Pilsner

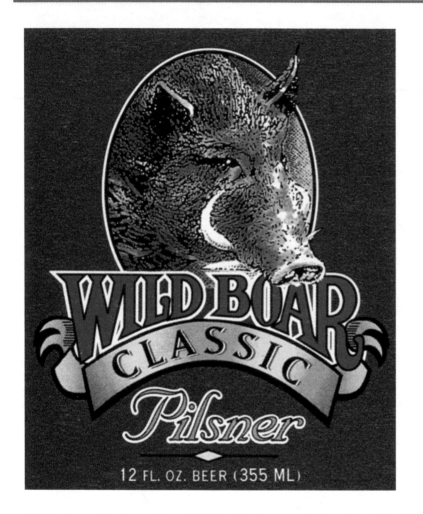

Dubuque Brewing Company
500 E. 4th St.
Dubuque, IA
  52001-2398
(319) 583-2042

Other Wild Boar Beers:
Special Amber
Wild Winter
Wild Wheat

First released in the spring of 1994, this is a true Bohemian (Czech)-style pilsner, with all the taste and quality associated with the traditional European brews. Only the finest carapils malt and Saaz hops are used, to give the beer a truly authentic Old World flavor. Saaz are arguably the world's most noble hops, and add a distinct floral and aromatic character. This fine pilsner was a gold medal winner in the 1994 World Beer Championships®.

Wild Goose Brewery
20 Washington St.
Cambridge, MD 21613
(410) 221-1121

Other Wild Goose Beers:
Snow Goose Winter Ale
Spring Wheat Ale
India Pale Ale
Amber Ale
Golden Ale

Wild Goose Porter is a classic representation of the traditional English style, which evolved from a pouring of stout and lager favored by train porters—hence its name. Looking almost black at first glance, Wild Goose Porter is a deep-reddish, smooth, creamy, and dry ale with hints of caramel, licorice, and coffee. Fresh Cascade, Willamette, Hallertau, Tettnang, and Kent Goldings hops build a velvety finish.

Windjammer Blonde Ale

Sea Dog Brewing Company
26 Front St.
Bangor, ME 04401
(207) 947-8004

Other Beers:
Old Gollywobbler
  Brown Ale
Old East India Pale
  Ale

The intense aromatics and full flavor of Cascade hops are balanced by the richness of traditional two-row British malted barley in Windjammer Blonde Ale to produce a blonde ale of uncompromising perfection. Top-fermented, the fruity palate and crisp finish bespeak its British origins.

Winter Iron

Irons Brewing Company
2027 W. Colfax Ave.
Denver, CO 80204
(303) 985-BEER

Other Beers:

Long Iron Bohemian
  Pilsner

Ironheart Red Ale

Dark Iron Chocolate
  Brown Ale

American Iron
  Amber Ale

Seven malt varieties give Winter Iron, a traditional dark beer, its creamy, dimpled head and deep garnet color. The rich, warming malt flavor carries a hint of dark chocolate. Winter Iron is the perfect winter warmer.

Winter Spice Ale

Stevens Point Brewery
2617 Water St.
Stevens Point, WI
 54481
(715) 344-9310

Other Point Beers:
Pale Ale
Special
Classic Amber
Bock
Maple Wheat

For your enjoyment during the winter season, Stevens Point Brewery has developed this handcrafted, limited-edition beer, called Point Winter Spice Ale. The exceptional taste is derived from a special recipe featuring cinnamon, nutmeg, two varieties of hops, and a caramel malt blend. Be sure to spice up your holiday season, every season, with Point Winter Spice Ale.

WIT Original

Spring Street Brewing Company
113 University Place
11th Floor
New York, NY 10003
(800) 948-8988

Other Beers:
WIT Amber
WIT Black

Five hundred years ago, Belgian brewers first perfected this unique beer style. During the 1700s more than thirty white-ale breweries prospered in Flemish-speaking lands. But by 1954 there was none, and the beer type was extinct. More recently, small Belgian and Dutch breweries have restored the style, and in the past few years this revival has gained momentum. WIT Original is an American rendition of the unfiltered white ale historically associated with the eastern provinces of Belgium. Brewed from wheat and spiced with Spanish orange peels and coriander, WIT Original is soft, light, and refreshing, without any bitterness or aftertaste.

Yellow Rose Pale Ale

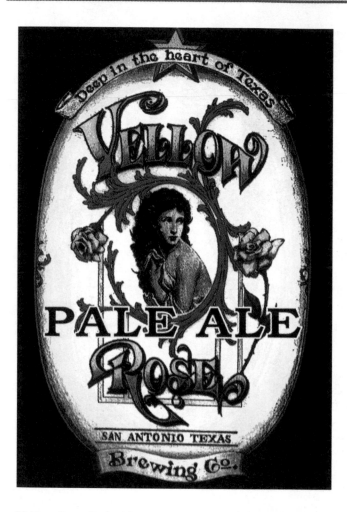

Yellow Rose Brewing Company
17201 San Pedro Ave.
San Antonio, TX
 78232
(210) 496-6669

Other Beers:
Vigilante Beer
Wildcatter's Crude
 Stout
Bubba Dog Beer
Cactus Queen Ale
Honcho Grande
 Brown Ale

Yellow Rose Pale Ale comes to you in limited quantities from a small South Texas brewery. It is brewed from Edwards Aquifer water, English barley malt, hops, and yeast. To ensure freshness, always keep refrigerated and consume within several weeks. Some haze or sediment may be normal in these fresh, unpasteurized, unfiltered beverages. Tastes best when enjoyed with good friends and good food!

Spanish Peaks Brewing Company

120 N. 19th Ave.
P.O. Box 3644
Bozeman, MT
  59772
(406) 585-0798

Other Beers:

Sweetwater Wheat
  Ale
Black Dog Ale
Honey Raspberry
  Ale

A traditional-style pale ale with a golden color and a full malty flavor that is surpassed only by the clean, crisp hop quality. The flowery hop aroma is enhanced by a generous portion of dry hopping. Brewed from pale malted barley, crystal, Munich, and Carastan malts, Pacific Northwest hops, water, and ale yeast. Chugwater Charlie Hill, M.H., is the name of the Labrador retriever shown on the Spanish Peaks label. "Chug," a title-winning black Lab, was selected to represent the fine breed that we honor with these award-winning Rocky Mountain ales.

Younger's Special Bitter

35 I.B.U.
12° PLATO
17° L
75 AA

ESTABLISHED 1988

Younger's Special Bitter
12 Fl. Oz.

Rogue Ales
3135 S.E. Ferry Slip
Rd. Newport, OR
  97365
(541) 867-3660

Other Beers:
American Amber Ale
Santa's Private
  Reserve
Oregon Golden Ale
Cran-n-Cherry Ale
Hazelnut Brown
  Nectar
Mocha Porter
Rogue-n-Berry Ale
Shakespeare Stout
St. Rogue Red Ale
Dead Guy Ale
Mexicali Rougue Ale
McRogue Scotch Ale
Old Crustacean
  Barleywine
Smoke Ale

This English-style special bitter won a silver medal in the 1996 World Beer Championships® and is considered to be one of America's five best ales by beer expert George Fix. Each thirty-barrel batch is a distinct micropiece, handmade by renowned brewer John Maier. Its complex flavor results from proprietary yeasts and the blending of the finest hops and malts available.

Zip City Brewing Company
3 W. 18th St.
New York, NY 10011
(212) 366-3333

Other Beers:
Zip City Altbier
Zip City Rauchbier
Zip City Dunkel
Zip City Pilsner

Zip City Brewing Company is celebrating its fifth anniversary in 1996. Located in Manhattan's historic Flatiron district, Zip City is the oldest continually operating brewery in the Big Apple. The brewpub, which began bottling for distribution in late 1995, features German-style lagers, ales, and wheat beers served unfiltered and unpasteurized, and menus of upscale pub fare. Zip City's Vienna-style amber lager is its most popular brand.

INDEX OF BREWERIES